Fishing the

Help Us Keep This Guide Up to Date

Every effort has been made by the author and editors to make this guide as accurate and useful as possible. However, many things can change after a guide is published—fish populations fluctuate, rules and regulations change, techniques evolve, sites and other facilities come under new management, Mother Nature asserts her will, and so on.

We would appreciate your comments concerning your experiences with this guide and how you feel it could be improved and kept up to date. While we may not be able to respond to all comments and suggestions, we'll take them to heart, and we'll also make certain to share them with the author. Please send your comments and suggestions to the following address:

> The Globe Pequot Press
> Reader Response/Editorial Department
> P.O. Box 480
> Guilford, CT 06437

Or you may e-mail us at:

> editorial@GlobePequot.com

Thanks for your input, and happy angling!

Fishing the
Texas Gulf Coast

An Angler's Guide to More Than
100 Great Places to Fish

CAPT. MIKE HOLMES

THE LYONS PRESS
GUILFORD, CONNECTICUT
AN IMPRINT OF THE GLOBE PEQUOT PRESS

The Lyons Press is an imprint of The Globe Pequot Press.

Interior photos © Mike Holmes
Text design by Casey Shain
Maps created by Marc Italia © Morris Book Publishing, LLC

Library of Congress Cataloging-in-Publication data is available on file.
ISBN 978-1-59921-237-1

Printed in the United States of America
10 9 8 7 6 5 4 3 2 1

To the late Harold Wells, who gave me most of my early writing assignments in *Gulf Coast Fisherman,* and to other outdoors writers who inspired and advised me—Stan Slaten, Ed Holder, Bob Stephenson Sr., Russell Tinsley, Hal Lyman, and George Heinold—all sadly deceased, and Charlie Waterman, who is still with us.
And also to Jim Kenworthy, who taught me secrets of the surf.

Mother Nature Asserts Her Will...

Many times in this text there are references to roads, businesses, and entire towns that have been heavily damaged by hurricanes or strong tropical storms. These severe weather events are a fact of life on the coast, and while they are necessary to renew and refresh the marine environment, they can take a terrible toll on residents. This has happened again in 2008, with Hurricane Dolly hitting the lower Laguna Madre area and, more recently, Hurricane Ike hitting the upper coast. Of the two, Ike was much more destructive—a Category II hurricane pushing a huge storm surge equal to that expected from a Cat IV. Bolivar Peninsula was devastated, with the majority of homes and businesses destroyed or badly damaged.

- As this is written, there is no ferry service from Bolivar to Galveston, due to damage to the ferry landings.
- Galveston itself lost much of its famous beach sand to erosion, and the fishing infrastructure of piers, bait camps, and other support businesses will not be back to "normal" for a long time.
- The Texas City Dike was completely submerged under the storm surge, all businesses destroyed, and the road damaged.
- Boats and marinas from Seabrook and Kemah to Freeport were badly treated, and County Road 257 from San Luis Pass to Surfside was left impassible for a stretch of about 4 miles.
- Even more sadly, more than thirty lives have been confirmed as lost so far, with many more people reported as missing and unaccounted for.

Most, if not all, of the damage will eventually be remedied. Just as these storms open up new channels and passes and flush out the back-bay systems and marshes, so do they force the rebuilding of man-made structures. Many of the changes will be for the better, although the cost in lives and property might seem to cancel this out.

Visitors must be patient, and check ahead before visiting the upper Texas coast. From just past Freeport to the south, however, Ike caused little or no damage, and Dolly was not as severe.

Contents

Overview

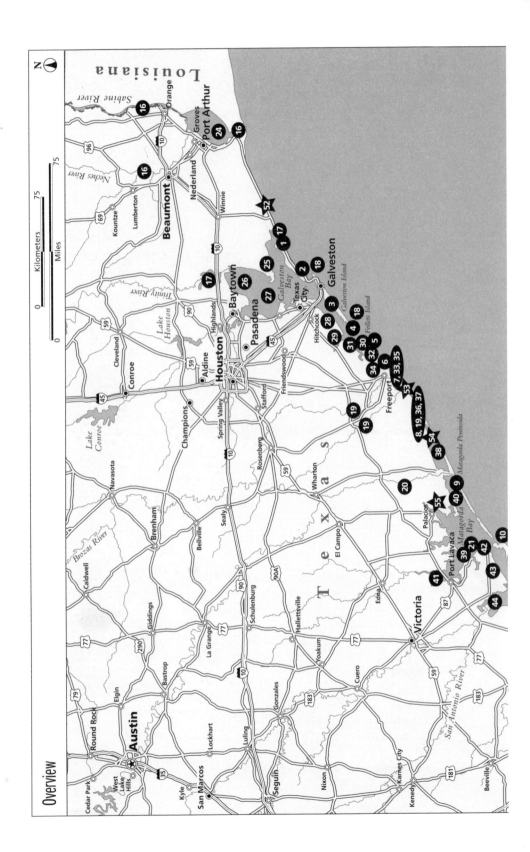

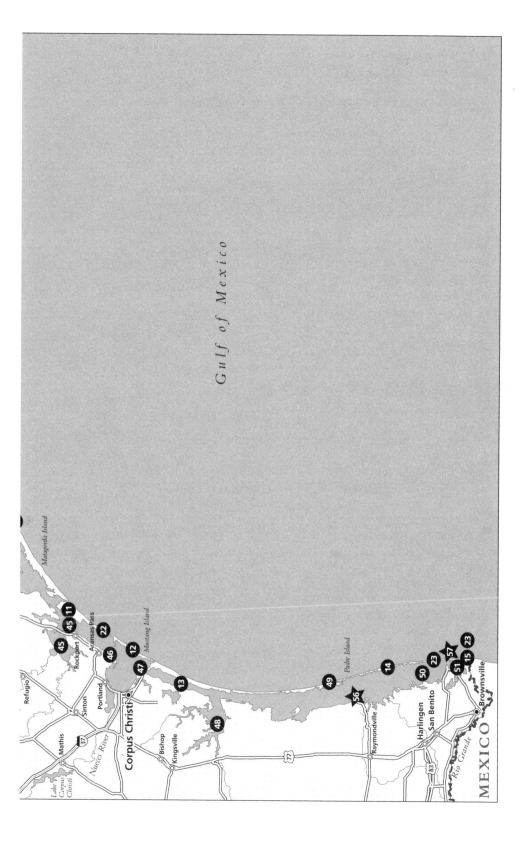

Acknowledgments

I would like to acknowledge Texas Parks & Wildlife for providing valuable information for this book, as well as the Hook-n-Line Map Company Inc. of Houston (www.hooknline.com), whose products were extremely helpful in detailing the Texas coast.

Introduction

Many people outside the state of Texas, and even some residents, think of images from TV or movies when the Lone Star State comes to mind. They picture pasturelands, oil fields, and arid deserts. Texas is actually so large that it encompasses these geological features and many more. We have the heavily forested eastern section of the state, vast areas of agricultural production in the central portion, rolling hills in the north approaching Oklahoma, a part of the Rocky Mountain chain in far west Texas, a lush coastal plain, citrus orchards in the Rio Grande Valley, and swamp-lined rivers on our border with Louisiana. And, yes, Texas does have a lot of cattle—in fact, when I write of saltwater fishing in Texas, I often refer to the areas as "The Cowboy Coast."

Texas has a coast, all right—367 miles of Gulf beaches, to be exact. Because we also have over a dozen major bay systems and many smaller bays and saltwater lakes, the total miles of tidewater shoreline is a staggering 3,300! Texas lays claim to the offshore waters of the Gulf of Mexico out to 9 nautical miles off our beaches, which brings the total amount of salt water to four million acres!

A total of fifteen major rivers flow through Texas or make up its boundaries, and a dozen of these empty into the Gulf itself or bay systems. Many smaller streams also terminate in salt water, providing a needed freshwater influx for marine creatures and potential fishing areas for recreational anglers.

Much of the Texas coast is sheltered by barrier islands—Galveston, Matagorda, Mustang, and Padre Islands being the largest. These offshore playgrounds offer both Gulf beach and protected bay shorelines. The passes between the islands and the mainland are not only excellent fishing areas, but also often provide deepwater access for boaters from the mainland or the back sides of the islands heading out to fish the Gulf.

In this guidebook we will examine the fishing opportunities on the Texas coast from the mouth of Sabine Pass on the border with Louisiana to the international border with Mexico at the mouth of the Rio Grande, including the major bay systems, offshore to the 9-nautical-mile limit of waters controlled by the state, and the saltwater portions of major river systems and other streams.

Visiting anglers and residents alike will find a tremendous amount of fishable water with public access, as Texas retains ownership of all shorelines for the people of the state. Besides Gulf beaches, there are miles of bayfront that can be driven to, so a boat is not always necessary for a productive fishing trip. Public and for-fee fishing piers extend into both Gulf and bays, and eight passes to the Gulf are protected by rock jetties that allow anglers on foot access to deeper waters.

The species of fish available range from panfish to sought-after game fish, from downright ugly and sometimes dangerous to exotic trophies approaching big-game classification. The "Big Three" of coastal waters here are redfish (red drum, or channel bass), speckled trout (spotted weakfish), and flounder, but there are also good

The view across the Freeport channel, from the Surfside Jetty to the Quintana Jetty, just before sunset.

eating fish like croaker, dangerous creatures such as sharks and rays, and trophy fish like tarpon and snook that are more often thought of as Florida residents.

For boaters fishing state waters offshore, and often also the "chunkers" who fish from piers, jetties, and the surf, the opportunity exists to catch red snapper, king mackerel, and ling (cobia)—the "Big Three" of offshore waters—as well as shark, tarpon, dolphin, and even the occasional sailfish. As one might expect from the miles of open beaches, surf fishing is excellent along this coast. Prime targets have always been "bull" redfish, jack crevalle, and a variety of sharks, but there are smaller species, such as gafftop catfish, for light-tackle anglers as well.

Professional guides are available to take newcomers fishing in the bays, offshore, and even down the beach on Padre Island. Residents are generally happy to share their thoughts on the best places and techniques, and coastal tackle and bait shops offer a wealth of "free" fishing advice.

Texas summers are hot, and the winters are short and mild. While the wind across the water from December through March can be uncomfortably cold, there is usually some area protected from a blow that is both fishable and fishy. Just about every month sees days of shirtsleeve weather, a major factor in the number of "Winter Texans" who abandon the chill of northern states for the Texas coast each year. RV parks on the southern portion of the coast are especially geared for this annual increase in our state's population. As in most areas along the water, visitors have little trouble finding great accommodations along the length of the entire coast.

Texas Parks & Wildlife is very aggressive in its rearing and stocking of several saltwater species at hatcheries up and down the coast. They have received the most

FISHING THE TEXAS GULF COAST

press for their efforts with red drum, but they also work with flounder, speckled trout, and even offshore species like cobia. The department has successfully introduced redfish and flounder into some freshwater lakes as well. While it is difficult to document the success of stocking programs in bays that ultimately connect to all the world's oceans, the programs have provided valuable information on the reproductive habits of the species involved, and this alone justifies their existence.

Fishing licenses support much of this research, as well as other programs, as do "special" permits, like the saltwater stamp required on the standard fishing license for both resident and nonresident anglers to fish in salt water. These licenses and stamps are available at most bait and tackle retailers and at Texas Parks & Wildlife offices.

With everything Texas has to offer the saltwater angler, it would be easy to spend a lifetime trying to fish all the areas for all available species—as I have. Should inshore fishing ever lose its challenge, or a change of pace be desired, there is the open Gulf of Mexico beyond, with fish from red snapper and grouper to marlin and tuna waiting to grab your bait. And even though the seafood on the Texas coast is beyond compare, if you'd like some variety in your diet, there are all those cows to provide prime steaks, briskets, and barbequed ribs!

Traveling Texas

Traveling the Texas coast is relatively simple, except for the sheer length of it. A small selection of major and minor roads carry a traveler from Louisiana to Mexico, usually with no traffic jams or annoying slowdowns. For first-time visitors, an explanation of the various classifications of roads and the speed limits on them could be helpful.

Interstate highways are those that pass through Texas from and to other states on its borders. Interstates are required to be controlled-access roadways with grade-separated interchanges. Some are four lanes but they are more often newer six-lane thoroughfares, many under constant construction and repair. The current speed limit on interstates outside of major urban areas is 70 mph. Inside designated metropolitan areas, such as Houston, the speed limit might be 55 or 60 mph, due to the determination that these are pollution-prone areas that can benefit from lower highway speeds.

U.S. highways are major city-to-city routes that connect large towns, other states, and Mexico. State highways are major routes not on the U.S. highway system, and they could be either two-lane or divided four-lane roads. Speed limits on these roads outside of cities and towns will generally be 70 mph. Business routes connect interstates, U.S. highways, and state highways to cities, as do loops and spurs.

Farm-to-market roads, ranch-to-market roads, and county roads are "minor" roadways providing service to rural areas. On farm-to-market roads, if a slow-moving tractor blocks your way, it has the right. All three will normally be two-lane roads. Speed limits can vary greatly in different counties—some will have a 70-mph limit, while others will be 45 mph. There are also park and recreation roads through state and national parks and recreation areas.

The speed limit on all Texas beaches, unless posted as lower, is 15 mph.

Interstate 10 comes in from the Louisiana border and connects Beaumont with Houston before heading straight west to San Antonio and beyond. Capillary roads head south off I-10 to the beach at High Island—where Texas Highway 87 fronts the beach to Galveston, via the Bolivar car ferry system—and Galveston Bay. Interstate 45 provides a direct route from Houston to Galveston Island, and Texas Highway 288 leads from Houston to Freeport. Freeport and Galveston are connected by Highway 257/3005/Bluewater Highway and the San Luis Pass Toll Bridge.

From Freeport, Texas Highway 35 is the roadway of choice to head south to Port O'Connor, Rockport/Fulton, and Corpus Christi, though locals might take Farm-to-Market Road 521 (FM 521) through Brazoria and Wadsworth as a shortcut that dodges Angleton, West Columbia, and Bay City. Texas Highway 60 from Bay City crosses FM 521 on its way to a dead end at Matagorda. From Corpus Christi, U.S. Highway 77 runs all the way to Brownsville on the Mexican border.

All of these road systems stay fairly close to the coastline and loop around major city congestion. Of course, in Texas, cities are generally spaced well apart.

Cautions

Be careful when fishing from the shorelines. Coastal grass beds and sand dunes are home to rattlesnakes, stingrays cruise the bays and surf, and the man-o'-war jellyfish that wash in regularly from the Gulf can impart a very painful sting. Experienced surf anglers keep meat tenderizer in their first-aid kits for these encounters. Strong currents in passes, river mouths, and the surf have the power to drown—and they do, each year. With normal caution, however, fishing Texas waters can be a very pleasurable experience.

How to Use This Guide

This book separates the fishing opportunities of the Texas coast into The Surf, Rivers and Passes, The Bays, and Near Offshore. All can be easily reached from the major roads, with usually only a minimal amount of travel on side roads. You can find detailed maps of the Texas coast at tackle shops and in the sporting goods section of big discount chains that are reasonably accurate on shoreline contours, stream courses, and the topography of the bays, including water depth. These maps are marked with suggested fishing spots and give the locations of boat ramps and bait camps. For anyone wanting to fish a particular area, a fishing map is much cheaper than hiring a guide, and it lasts longer than a guided trip.

I have not listed tackle shops or fishing guide services, because they both come and go fairly often. I have, however, mentioned some bait camps, as these usually change hands rather than shutting down completely. Since fishing regulations often change, they are only mentioned briefly. Before hitting the water, it would be advisable to either visit a major tackle center or call the nearest Texas Parks & Wildlife office for updated requirements. Guide services advertise in fishing magazines and coastal newspapers and in tackle shops.

Map Legend

Interstate Highway	══⟨64⟩══	Lake/Reservoir	
U.S. Highway	══⟨13⟩══	River	
State Highway	══⟨316⟩══	Swamp/Marsh	
Farm-to-Market Roads	┈⟨562⟩┈	Fishing Site	❷ ⭐56
International border	▪▪ ▪▪▪ ▪▪▪ ▪▪▪	State Historical Battleground Site	
State border	▪ ▪▪ ▪ ▪▪ ▪ ▪▪ ▪ ▪▪	Airport	⤬
Wildlife Refuge	⌐ ⌐	City	◉
		Large town	◎
Wildlife Management Impounds Area	▨	Town	○

Common Coastal Texas Fish Species

This variety of Texas inshore species includes back drum and redfish (center), as well as (counterclockwise, from the bottom) speckled trout, sand trout, and croaker. All were caught fishing at night under lights on Chocolate Bayou.

Texas is blessed to be home to many species of saltwater fish that are fun to catch, good to eat, and beautiful to behold. We also have some that are mean, ugly, and downright dangerous. Truly a mix of "The Good, the Bad, and the Ugly," but some of the ugly fish are the most challenging to catch.

Most inshore species are here and hungry year-round, though their habits may change with the seasons. Some inshore species migrate to the deep waters of the Gulf of Mexico during winter, and many of the migratory pelagic fish, which roam the waters just off the beach, either go south for the winter or head to deeper water themselves. Still others, mostly residents of deep, cold water in the Gulf, might actually come closer to shore in winter.

I will not go into Latin names here, just the common names that visitors might know some of these fish by and what they are called in Texas. A bit of natural history also seems appropriate to help the angler determine where to look for each species, what bait to try, and the proper tackle to use. Because regulations and license requirements change from year to year, the angler should get the most up-to-date information before heading out for the water.

We will begin our examination of what is available to anglers—and when—with the three most popular bay species: speckled trout, redfish, and flounder.

Speckled Trout—Nothing Weak about This Fish!

Well, actually, there is something weak about our "trout," and that would be its common name. Early Texans, like pioneers everywhere, tended to identify the new creatures they encountered with common species back home. The shiny, graceful, slender fish that they found in Texas bays and in the surf looked like the freshwater trout some of them were used to, but they are actually more properly known as spotted weakfish. Several varieties of weakfish roam the Gulf and Atlantic coasts of the United States. The spotted ones are not the largest—the common weakfish of the Atlantic takes that honor—but they are not the smallest either.

Speckled trout, or "specks," are common all along the Texas coast, very sporty on light tackle, fairly easy to catch, excellent table fare, and grow large enough to be considered "trophies" to a whole legion of anglers. Silver-white with tiny black spots, larger specks have two big teeth in their mouth, which is bright yellow inside. They feed on everything from shrimp to large mullet—and even smaller speckled trout.

The first nice trout I ever caught came on a surf rod near San Luis Pass, on Galveston Island. I was actually trying to hook a big redfish, and was using a double drop leader with strips cut from a small shark for bait. When the rod bowed down and I reeled in my catch, I had a rare double—a small sharp-nosed shark on one

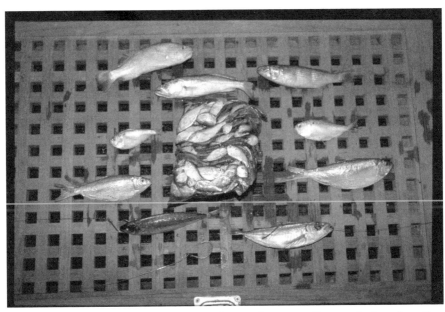

Common species used for bait include croaker, sand trout, mullet, menhaden, threadfin shad, piggy perch, and cigar minnows.

hook, and a 5-pound speckled trout on the other. When word of that catch got out, anglers all over Galveston were seeking sharks for trout bait—sort of a turnaround of normal hunter and quarry.

Live shrimp are always a plus when fishing for speckled trout, and most experienced anglers either live-line them on small hooks with a light or no leader around jetty rocks or pilings, or fish them under a popping cork with a small split shot—sized according to current and bait size—between the float and the hook. Popping corks were developed in Texas for trout fishing. The "cork" is usually actually a tapered cylinder of Styrofoam, either split down the side or drilled down the middle for the line to go through. A peg longer than the cork slides in to hold the line in position for the desired depth—which might be 6 inches or 6 feet, depending on water depth. The cork has a scooped upper face that, when "popped" by twitching the rod, makes a sort of blurping sound that we hope simulates the sound of a trout engulfing a shrimp on or near the surface. Since the trout are school fish that feed in groups, they use sound as well as scent or sight to locate prey.

Other good live baits for speckled trout are small shad and mullet, piggy perch, and any other small baitfish. Especially good for larger trout are fairly big croakers, sand trout, mullet, or skipjacks—up to a foot long. Good dead baits include chunks of mullet or shad, squid, fresh shrimp, and, of course, pieces of small shark.

Look for trout where there are signs of bait, especially in clear water. Deeper areas close to shallow flats, oyster reefs, channels, streams running into bay systems, around passes, in the surf, along jetty rocks, and in residential canals and marina harbors—speckled trout might be found in all these places.

The Texas state record speckled trout of 15.6 pounds was caught in Baffin Bay, off the Laguna Madre, on a fly rod in 2002 and released. Baffin has produced the last few state record trout, but several years ago a 16-pound-plus trout was documented from the Seabrook Flats off Galveston Bay. It won the trout division in the IGFA fishing contest that year, but the angler was leery of politics and publicity, and did not submit it for state record consideration.

The Redfish Beats Its Own Drum!

The redfish is really more of a copper/bronze in color, and usually has one large black spot near its tail. The red's underslung mouth marks it as mostly a bottom feeder—though it can be found chasing bait on the surface. On the East Coast these fish are known as channel bass, and in Florida they're more often called red drum.

There are actually two classes of redfish. The young of the species, under 20 pounds by the standards of the group I used to surf fish with, are often referred to as "rat reds," and these are the redfish found in the bay systems. The adult spawners, or "bull reds," live in the Gulf and range from 20 to 50-plus pounds. Tackle, bait, and techniques are very different when fishing for rats versus bulls.

Smaller redfish are excellent light-tackle adversaries, and will take a variety of live and dead baits as well as artificial lures. They will actually hit surface lures with abandon when feeding on schooling mullet, and they like plastic shrimp imitations as well. Gold spoons are a traditional favorite lure for reds. These fish like to feed in shallow water, where small crabs actually make up a large part of their diet. Reds "tailing" in water so shallow their backs and tails are exposed are great targets for fly fishers, and many experts rank them with bonefish as prime flats-fishing sport. In deeper portions of the bays and up tidal streams, redfish will be found on or near shell reefs or gravel points. While they will take live baits, reds have such a good sense of smell that they sometimes prefer dead bait that is easier for them to locate. Shrimp and finger mullet are most popular, but squid will work, too.

Bull reds rarely enter the bays but can be found at times in passes and river mouths. Most are taken by anglers off jetties, beachfront piers, and in the surf itself. Since these are strong, heavy fish, stout tackle is needed. Long rods are used to make casts as far as possible from the beach, and 30- or 40-pound-test line is needed to withstand the abrasion of sand and shell. Anglers in the surf usually use several rods that are placed in sand-spike rod holders while waiting for a fish to hit.

Most big reds are taken on live or dead bait, with mullet being the first choice, but shad, sand trout, croaker, skipjack, and squid are also used. Circle hooks are gaining popularity because they are virtually self-setting and almost always hook in the corner of the mouth. This is important for fish that must be released. The big reds over 28 inches in length are protected, and they must be tagged with the tag on the saltwater fishing license. Only one fish per season is allowed, but an extra tag for an additional fish will be given if the first tag is returned to Texas Parks & Wildlife.

Adult reds taken from the surf will run from 20 to 40 pounds. The state record stood at 51.25 pounds for many years, but it was broken in 2000 by a fish weighing a whopping 59.5 pounds that was caught off a beachfront pier.

Flounder—Their Taste Is Anything but Flat!

The most common flatfish found in Texas waters is the Southern flounder, and it is prized for its wonderful flavor and the amount of meat it provides more than for its fighting ability. Flounder are challenging quarry on a rod and reel, but mostly because it can be difficult to entice them to hit. Unlike most fish that hunt their prey, flounder usually lie in wait on the bottom, camouflaged by their low profile and coloration, digging into the sand or mud and ambushing their food as it moves by. Because of this, look for flounder near moving water—outflows of canals, streams, or ditches, and near drop-offs during a moving tide.

Properly fishing for flounder means moving your bait or lure slowly over the bottom, hoping it passes near enough to a succulent flatfish to get its attention. When using jigs, skip them to kick up puffs of mud, and with live or dead bait, position a light sinker several inches in front of the bait to do the same thing. Good baits for flounder include shrimp and small mullet, but the most prized is the Gulf killifish, commonly known as the mud minnow. Of course, there is always an exception to every rule, and by casting bait out and just letting it sit, I have caught many nice flounder, including one over 6 pounds that swallowed a big piece of mullet on a large circle hook meant to entice an alligator gar.

Because flounder are prized mostly as a food fish and they are present in large numbers, it is legal to spear them at night with a gig of some sort. Flounder giggers either wade with a lantern equipped with a reflector to intensify and aim the beam, or they use specially rigged shallow-draft boats with lights on the front and often some sort of motorized fan on the back to move them slowly over shallow water while they scan the bottom for signs of fish.

New flounder anglers will soon discover that the fish has a very small internal body cavity for its size, maximizing the amount of meat yielded. They may also be surprised to see that both its eyes are on the same side of its body—the dark-colored side that faces up. The bottom of the flounder is white. While normally thicker on the top half, both sides offer good eating. Flounder grilled, baked, or scored and fried is one of the most delicious fish on the Gulf coast.

The Texas state record flounder weighed 13 pounds and was caught in Sabine Lake. A flounder this size would feed several hungry people—for more than one meal!

Panfish—Easy to Catch, Easy to Love

There are many smaller inhabitants of Texas coastal waters that do not reach sizes large enough to be considered "sport fish" but are prized nonetheless for their eating qualities. Most of these fish are relatively easy to find and catch, and most have no bag or size limits to worry amount.

In this category we have the croaker, which is a smaller member of the same general family as the redfish; sand trout, a smaller weakfish that in larger sizes is found in the Gulf and referred to as "Gulf trout"; whiting, which is very similar to croaker; the very tasty pompano; sheepshead; small versions of black drum; and the gafftop catfish, which should never be confused with the common hardhead catfish that is considered unfit to eat.

Dead shrimp or squid and light tackle are generally all that is necessary to catch some form of panfish, just about anywhere there is access to salt water.

Bruisers—These Fish Fight Back! Black Drum and Alligator Gar

On the Texas coast, it is possible for shore-based anglers to hook some very large fish. While bull reds and tarpon can be caught from piers or the surf, other big fish will be found in bay systems, even up tidal streams, offering a chance for anglers to tangle with big game for relatively small bucks.

The black drum is the redfish's ugly cousin. Although small drums can be good eating, the flesh of the larger ones is coarse and often inhabited by worms. Big drums—over 30 inches in length—are protected and must be released anyway.

While spending most of their lives in the deeper water offshore, black drums make a midwinter spawning run into the bay systems. Anglers intercept them in passes, usually, but they can be found at some recognized hot spots inside the bays, including the Texas City Dike—a long jetty-like protrusion into Galveston Bay that can be driven on and has a fishing pier at the end that extends almost to the Houston Ship Channel. Other recognized drum hot spots are the bank and pier at Sea Wolf Park, near the Bolivar ferry landing on the Galveston side, the Galveston jetties, and the piers along the Galveston beachfront and at San Luis Pass.

While big drums will eat mullet or large dead shrimp, they prefer blue crabs. Drum anglers remove the outer shell and quarter the crabs, hooking them through the leg holes. Circle hooks are popular because of their self-setting qualities and the ease of releasing fish. The state record black drum weighed 61 pounds and drums over 40 pounds are commonly caught, but since they have a sluggish nature when hooked and rarely make long runs, they can be bested on much lighter tackle than that required for a big redfish.

Another heavyweight found in the bays and tidal waters is the prehistoric-looking alligator gar. The 'gator gar is technically a freshwater species but has a high tolerance for salt water. When beach seining was legal in Texas, gars were sometimes captured in these nets near High Island, and gill netters would find them in most major bays. Because of their size and strength—the saltwater state record gar, taken in Galveston Bay, weighed 186.19 pounds (the freshwater record, taken in the Rio Grande on a trotline, weighed in at over 256 pounds!)—most big gars are captured on heavy tackle by anglers who know what they are fishing for. There actually are anglers who consider the gar a great sport fish. They have great strength, will often jump almost clear of the water, and have a boney mouth hard to set a hook in—qualities that earned them the nickname "poor man's tarpon."

For a More Exotic Flavor: Striped Bass, Blue Catfish, Tripletail, Tarpon, and Snook

There are other fish in Texas inshore waters that are not as commonly encountered, including fish more often found in Texas freshwater, such as striped bass and blue

This 14-inch tarpon was taken from a school chasing bait in Chocolate Bayou in winter.

catfish. Both of these species are occasionally found in brackish streams and even in the bay systems.

Then there is the tripletail, an odd-looking creature whose dorsal and under fins extend as far back as the tail. The tripletail is a flat, wide-bodied fish similar in shape to the freshwater crappie. They reach large sizes for a bay fish—the state record, which came from Matagorda Bay, weighed 33.5 pounds—and are often found in offshore waters under any type of drifting material. I once watched a tripletail follow a discarded water cooler almost to the beach in calm surf. The only inshore water where tripletails are common is Matagorda Bay, and no one seems to have any idea why. Tripletails fight hard and are excellent on the table, so most anglers consider them a pleasant bonus.

The tarpon is the trophy fish of inshore waters. Though more often found in the Gulf, the "silver king" does enter passes and river mouths, and it can be taken from the surf and beachfront piers, like the 210.7-pound state record caught off a Galveston pier in 2006. I have seen "baby" tarpon far up a coastal bayou chasing baitfish, an indication that these fish possibly spawn in Texas waters. The tarpon is famous for its powerful runs and exciting jumps.

Many anglers might think a trip to Florida or Central America is necessary to catch snook, but these tropical gamesters have made a comeback in extreme south Texas waters over the last decade. They are the target of bay guides in the Lower Laguna Madre and are found around the Port Isabel/Brownsville jetties. In 1982, during a rare fish-killing freeze on the Texas coast, a snook was found barely alive in Chocolate Bayou, off West Bay—much farther north than snook were thought to live.

Watch Out for These! Sharks and Stingrays

There are a few fish most anglers would rather not run into on the average fishing trip. Sharks are always a concern in salt and brackish water, and Texas waters have many varieties that are found inshore and in the surf. Small sharks are great sport on light tackle and are as good to eat as many more traditional "food" species. Wire leaders are necessary to capture even small sharks, and always be wary of their teeth. Experienced wade fishers who work the surf and areas near passes keep captured specks and reds on a long stringer so that a hungry shark who wants them for a snack doesn't get too close to legs and feet!

Several subspecies of stingrays in various sizes are found in bays and the surf. The state record Atlantic stingray weighed only 10.75 pounds, but the record Southern stingray went 246 pounds! Stingrays fight differently on a rod and reel, like a large bird flapping its wings under the water, but they are very strong and have a habit of sucking on the bottom to resist the pressure of the line. They are good to eat, but most that are caught are hooked by accident. I have seen rays caught on surf rods to 140 pounds, though my personal best was closer to 70.

What most concerns wading anglers in regard to rays is not stepping on them. There is a serrated barb at the base of the ray's tail that is covered with a poison that causes a wound from the barb to be extremely painful. The ray can't use this weapon to attack—it is strictly for defense—so unless an angler steps on the fish

Big stingrays are worthy adversaries—and good eating—but they should be handled carefully.

and drives it in with his or her own weight, there isn't much to fear. Shuffling your feet along the bottom is recommended to push a ray aside or scare it instead of stepping on it.

Beyond the Breakers: Offshore Species

Although many—if not most—of the same species found in Texas bays will be found in the Gulf waters just off the beach, there are some other fish rarely or never seen in the bays. King mackerel, Spanish mackerel, ling (cobia), jack crevalle, bonito (little tunny), and even red snapper can be found in the Gulf waters out to the 9 nautical miles under state regulation.

Tackle, Boats, and Beach Transportation for the Texas Coast

The dock behind a seafood restaurant in Port Isabel is occupied by the types of shallow-water fishing boats favored by south Texas anglers.

While just about any type of fishing tackle can be found in use on the Gulf coast, from fly rods to spinning gear to the tin cans with line wrapped around them used by Mexican fishers below the border, a particular rod and reel combination has been developed over the decades that works especially well for fishing the Texas coast. A visitor who is serious about Texas fishing can certainly blend in with—and get more "insider" advice from—the local pros when he or she is armed with the "proper" gear to begin with.

Besides the rod and reel outfit, there are certain terminal rigs and lures that are favored here—because they work. This is not to say that a fly rod expert can't put his favorite tackle to good use or a freshwater angler can't use her bass-fishing tackle to catch trout and reds in the bays, but for general everyday fishing, it is often wise to go with what locals use when they hit the water.

A variety of water conditions might be encountered by a boating angler in Texas, from inches-deep flats to deep bays that can get as rough as the Gulf under a bad wind. No single boat type will handle all these conditions, but there are compromise craft that will do yeoman's service under most conditions and more specialized vessels that were designed and built for a certain narrow range of operation. One of these, the shallow-water "scooter," is a unique Texas invention.

Rods and Reels

The single most common tackle outfit in use on the Texas coast is the popping rod. Developed primarily for casting and working live shrimp under a popping cork, the rod will be from 6½ to 7½ feet in length, with a "soft" tip section that bends under a load to cast farther, a stronger butt section for fighting large fish, and a two-handed grip to enable the angler to put more muscle behind his cast. Graphite rods have become quite popular, but fiberglass "sticks" still work well.

The most popular reel for this outfit for many, many years was the red Garcia Ambassador 5000–6000 series level-wind bait-casting reel. Newer reels have largely replaced the "red ones" in recent years for bass fishing, but the simpler, basic baitcaster is still a better choice for saltwater use, as it resists the intrusion of salt and sand better. Good, nearly new models can be found very reasonably priced in resale shops and at garage sales. With 12- to 17-pound-test monofilament line and mounted on a good popping rod, these reels will not only cast live bait, but also both hard and soft lures or light bottom rigs. They will handle trout, reds, and flounder in the bays as well as light offshore fishing for kings and snapper—and can even give a tarpon a run for his money.

When winds are light and the water is shallow, fly tackle can be an excellent tool for tailing redfish and shallow-feeding trout. Because reds can get hefty, an 8- or 9-weight rod is recommended, with a floating line and a reel capable of handling a good amount of backing. Some large flounder have been taken on fly rods, and they can be excellent for panfish as well.

Some anglers prefer spinning tackle, and it can be used to great effect in Texas waters, especially when tossing light lures or live baits with little or no weight. Spinning gear came to the Gulf coast later than the east and west coasts, but because of the great influx of new residents from these other areas, it is now more commonly seen than a couple of decades ago and is widely sold throughout the state at tackle shops.

For serious surf fishing for big reds, jacks, and sharks, heavier gear is required. Pier anglers use stiff rods up to 10 feet in length because they do not have to cast as far, but a beach angler might go to a 14-foot surf stick with a more flexible tip section to let her heave her baits out as far as possible. The long rod also helps in fighting a big fish from the beach, as the constant flex and pressure it provides strains the fish much like a fly rod does. Conventional reels such as the classic Penn Squidder, Jigmaster, or Senator models in 3/0 and 4/0 sizes have long been popular. The 7000 series Garcia models also have advocates. Heavy-duty spinning tackle is popular in the surf, too. In a pinch, though, the basic popping rod can be used, especially for lighter fish.

An alternative to both conventional and spinning reels is the Alvey sidecast reel, from Australia. Looking like a big fly reel hanging beneath the rod on a very short butt, these are single-action reels with a 1:1 retrieve ratio. Line retrieve speed is determined by the size of the spool, and they come in several models with different spool sizes. The reels have handles on the right-hand side, use star drags, and are completely constructed of fiberglass, stainless steel, and a few brass bushings. Removal of the nut that secures the handle and drag wheel allows the spool to be taken off the driveshaft for easy rinsing and cleaning.

Sidecast reels resemble the "mooching" reels used to bait fish for salmon in the Northwest, with one serious difference: pushing a lever just under the reel seat releases the reel to swivel to the side, so that line peels off the spool like a spinning reel. When the reel is swiveled back and locked in retrieval position, it now behaves like a conventional right-hand retrieve reel. Because of the large spool diameters—the most popular models are 5½ to 6 inches, but some run larger—each time a "loop" of line peels off, it is a significant length, and there is very little resistance.

For many years Alvey reels held all the distance-casting world records, and they are still very competitive, even though tackle from most other manufacturers used in these competitions these days is not exactly standard surf-fishing gear. Sidecast reels do require some getting used to for experienced anglers, but beginners find them very simple to learn. The short butt also takes some adjustment. For one thing, it doesn't sit in a sand spike as well as a longer butt, but this can be remedied with a modified rod holder with a slot down the side the reel will be on. I did tests a few years ago on the same surf rod with two reel seats, casting several times with a sidecast reel and several times with a Penn Squidder. The sidecast reel cast considerably farther, and at the time I was very competent with a Squidder.

The serious shark fishers who haunt the beaches, jetties, and piers on summer nights might be found using stiff big-game-class boat rods, reels in the 6/0 to 12/0 size class, 80-pound lines, heavy cable leaders, and 20-pound jackfish for bait.

Terminal Tackle

The easiest way to spot a novice angler on the Texas coast is by his ready-made rig off the tackle shop rack, consisting of heavy (usually blue) monofilament or braided wire cable. It will be a two- or three-hook rig, with heavy crimps and lots of red beads. When you see these rigs for sale, run—do not walk—away from them as fast as you can! Sure, hardhead catfish will bite dead bait fished on these rigs, but that is exactly why these undesirable critters are called "tourist trout" by the locals.

The popping cork rig mentioned above is excellent for trout, reds, panfish, and even flounder under some circumstances. It utilizes a popping cork—an elongated cone (usually made of Styrofoam) with a scooped top—that can be "popped" by twitching the rod to imitate the sound of trout feeding on shrimp or baitfish on the surface. It can also be used to simply suspend the bait at a proper depth, like most fishing floats. A monofilament or fluorocarbon leader of no more than 20-pound test is best, with both the cork and a weight appropriate to the size of the bait and the conditions of the water—current strength, depth, etc.—on the leader and the whole rig attached to the main fishing line with a light snap swivel.

For live-lining shrimp or small baitfish, use the same leader material and either no weight at all or just enough to allow casting and getting the bait down in the water column. When bottom fishing—for, say, flounder or maybe redfish—a slip sinker is often used, letting it slide along the leader but not all the way to the bait.

Here is where a small crimp or bead for a stop is helpful. The slip sinker allows the fish to pick up the bait without feeling a lot of resistance, and it allows either dead or live bait to move freely in the current.

Surf anglers use 60- to 120-pound-test single-strand wire leaders because sand and shell can cut mono, as can the teeth of even small sharks. My favorite rig is a single drop, using a strong three-way swivel halfway down a 3-foot leader to lead one piece of wire about 12 inches long to a circle hook. I often have a second, smaller hook sliding on this wire to allow for a hook in both ends of the bait. The remaining eye of the swivel has a similar length of wire leading to either a "surf spider" weight or a pyramid sinker. The spider weight used on the Texas coast weighs 4 to 8 ounces, depending on water conditions, and is cast from lead with heavy copper tines sticking out, like a small anchor. This is the only type of sinker that will hold bottom in heavy surf, though pyramids will work in more moderate conditions. When a big fish picks up the bait held by a spider weight, the resistance of the sinker will help set the hook before it pulls loose.

Treble hooks have long been the standard on the Texas coast for trout and redfish when using bait and on artificial plugs. More recently there has been a movement to single hooks, as they are less damaging to the fish when release might be desirable, such as with undersize catches. Small circle hooks are also becoming more popular, as this type of hook is self-setting and almost always hooks the fish in the corner of its mouth, making hook removal much easier and successful releases much more likely.

Artificial Lures

Artificial offerings are considered more sporting by some anglers, and they certainly simplify the process of casually pursuing fish. The same lure can be cast all day, or a fisher can change lures to his—or her—heart's content. When bait is scarce, lures are easy to find, and hardheads, piggy perch, and other small "bait stealers" do not bother lures. While the art of bait fishing—catching or selecting bait, keeping it in fishable condition, and presenting it properly—is certainly not easy, at least a fish knows it is supposed to eat a natural bait. With lures, the angler has to select the right offering, present and "work" it properly, and cast it well enough to get it where the fish can find it.

The basic lures for Texas coastal fishing are normally either soft plastic imitations of shrimp or small baitfish, or hard lures designed to imitate mullet or other larger targets. The first plastic baits were generically called "touts" after the brand name of a shrimp-tail imitation which spawned many imitations of its own. The shrimp-tail jig is still a favorite lure, and it is especially easy for freshwater anglers to master, as it is fished on a lead-head jig just like the "grubs" used for bass fishing. There are also versions of this lure type that imitate various eels and saltwater worms, as well as shad imitations. These lures are economical, easy to use, and effective. Smaller jigs are sometimes rigged in tandem, two on a leader. Plastic jig tails can also be fished under a popping cork; in fact, a type of cork designed especially for this use is marketed with the addition of a couple of beads to make a rattling noise in addition to the cork's "pop."

Another type of jig usually rigged in tandem is the small nylon-skirted "spec rig." These are very deadly on smaller fish, like panfish, but will also fool a larger speck or red.

The original baitfish-imitating hard lure is the spoon. Johnson Sprites in silver for trout and gold for redfish prevail on the Texas coast, but other brands are also used. Spoons cast well in the wind, making them a good choice for surf casting, and they also excel for dredging fish out of deep holes.

For decades the gold standard for plastic plugs was the Mirrolure 52M series, a slow-sinking mullet imitation with a red back, white underside, and gold sides. More big speckled trout have been taken on this plug than any other. New lures from Mirrolure have a more controlled sink rate, with an eye in the nose of the plug instead of the top of the head to change the angle of pull, and topwaters are also quite popular. The technique known as "walking the dog," borrowed from bass fishing, is very effective on reds as well as trout. Freshwater bass lures, like the lipped deep-diving lures of the Rebel/Rapala type, are very effective on bay species as well.

Because the old saying that most lures are designed more to catch anglers than to catch fish is very true, all you really need to catch lots of fish on the Texas coast are a handful of shrimp tails, a few spoons, and a couple of old-style Mirrolures.

Boats

As mentioned at the beginning of this chapter, Texas bays run from only a few inches to as much as 20 feet deep. The average, statewide, is probably somewhere around 4 to 7 feet. There are not only deeper channels running through most bays,

These anglers are netting a nice flounder in the Brownsville Ship Channel, near the jetty on the Boca Chica side. Note the shallow-water boat employed.

but also shallow reefs and sandbars. In larger bays, when the wind is up, waves can be dangerous for smaller boats. Conversely, the shallow bays can strand a larger boat high and dry. Many anglers prefer to wade for fish in shallow—and sometimes even not-so-shallow—water and use a boat mainly for transportation to and from fishing spots. For fishing the passes and jetties, however, a seaworthy vessel that can handle the threat of rough water and carry a few anglers and their gear is required.

Boats are nearly always a compromise, and many types can be successfully utilized. Bass anglers can use their lake boats in the bays and around jetties in good weather. Larger boats more suited for offshore use can fish the jetties and passes and transport anglers down the Intracoastal Waterway to hot wade-fishing locations.

For running shallow bays, craft from aluminum johnboats to airboats might be used. Anglers in the Laguna Madre developed a flat-bottomed "sled" type of boat that could float in very shallow water and figured out how to mount an outboard high enough so that only the propeller was touching the water. The "scooter" boat has evolved a lot in the past few years, with low-water pickups to provide water for the engine, cavitation plates on the lower units to force the water flow back down on the prop, and raised platforms fore and aft for casting and poling platforms. These boats are commercially constructed now by several local builders and stretch to 20 feet in length or even longer. They are capable of getting on plane in just inches of water and skimming over flats most other boats would flounder on (pardon the pun). While still most popular on the lower coast, scooters are also now used on the rest of the Texas coast as well. These are "fun" boats, by anyone's standards.

A whole breed of "bay boats" similar to the genre of bass boats have also developed and are quite popular in Texas. Most of these are semi-V hulls, 20 to 25 feet in length, and have a fairly wide beam. While not as shallow-water capable as a scooter, they will run in most bays and can cross open water in a wind.

As mentioned above, the flat-bottomed aluminum johnboat is very popular in Texas bays. These craft are quite often "tricked out" for specialty use, with things like rails and lights on the bow for flounder gigging, and sometimes small fan-type motors, like those used on ultralight aircraft, mounted on the stern to slowly push the boat over shallows while searching for flatfish. They are often also equipped with fantails with live bait wells built in, and steps for easy access for waders. Because these boats' weak point is that the rivets that normally hold them together will eventually loosen after years of pounding over a washboard bay surface, several locally built brands are welded instead of riveted. Center consoles are added, and fairly large engines are used. Some bay boats now use special saltwater electric "trolling" motors.

In the "old days," bait camps along the coast commonly rented small skiffs to anglers, who either rowed them out or brought their own small outboards to use. Some still do.

Occasionally you will see an inflatable boat on the Texas coast, and they are not stared at as much as when I had my first one back in the late 1970s. Inflatables are very useful for running shark baits out in the surf, either when powered by oars or a small outboard engine. They can also be used to fish short distances from shore. I have fished and run inflatables from an 8-foot dinghy to an 18-foot model rated for up to 75 hp. The inflatable I have had the most experience with is a 10-footer with a 15-hp outboard. This type of boat is very good for people who have limited storage space, as they can be deflated to take up less room. The newer rigid-hull inflatables are even better, as they have a hard-bottomed fiberglass hull, often with chambers in the hull that fill with water at rest (increasing stability), with an inflatable tube surrounding it.

Practice Safe Boating

While a decent bay boat can be used to venture short distances offshore in very good weather, please do not push your luck and challenge doubtful conditions. In anything over a slight chop, a good deep-V hull of 20 feet or more is a better choice, though a boat like this is marginal for regular offshore use. If using a boat intended for calmer conditions, be patient and pick your days to fish. If it is too rough, stay in protected waters. Even on those millpond days, carry all required safety equipment, let someone know your plans, and have some type of communications device onboard.

Beach Transportation

Anglers who are serious about surf fishing will need to consider some form of transportation other than the family sedan for travel down the beaches. Much can be done with a standard two-wheel-drive pickup truck—which often is the family sedan in Texas! The next step is a four-wheel-drive vehicle, but there are other options. There aren't as many of the VW-powered beach buggies as there once were, but they will really go in soft sand. Where legal, three- and four-wheel ATVs can be trailered to the beach and then used to travel farther than the vehicle towing them can go. Anglers with disabilities or who simply don't care to walk as much can use modified electric golf carts with lifted frames, larger tires, and often more powerful motors to get to their favorite spot.

For more casual fishing, however, there are public parking areas on or just off paved roads within walking distance of prime surf casting. This is a sport that can be as easy, or as involved, as you want it to be.

The Surf

Surf fishing is the ultimate act of man communing with nature, one on one. It requires no boat, no electronic gizmos, and only basic tackle. Bait can often be captured on the spot, and a variety of types will do. Fishing from the beach can be a solitary sport or a family affair—it is perfectly suited to either. Equipment can be minimal—just a single rod and reel will get you started—or very involved. Dedicated surf anglers use long rods and special reels to cast their baits far past the breakers, often fishing several rods held in pipe "sand spikes" near the water's edge while waiting for a fish to bite.

A four-wheel-drive vehicle is helpful to reach off-the-beaten-path spots, but not necessary to just have fun. Some anglers use surf-launched boats to carry baits farther out in an effort to hook big sharks, tarpon, and other glamorous species, while others wade with light tackle and lures for speckled trout and Spanish mackerel.

Driving and camping on the beach is still permissible in some areas, but more and more beachfront cities are restricting access and charging a fee to park on the sand. They cannot, however, restrict pedestrians from walking—or fishing—on the beaches, which are by law the property of the people of the state of Texas.

A four-wheel-drive vehicle is often necessary to reach the best surf-fishing spots. This is the Brown Cedar side of the Sargent Cut.

Sabine Pass to San Luis Pass

The main artery of pavement serving the eastern Texas coastline is Highway 87, which runs out of Port Arthur down the eastern shore of Sabine Lake and across the Intracoastal Waterway (ICW) to the small town of Sabine Pass. From there, Highway 87 had historically turned west and traveled just off the beach all the way to Galveston Island. Many hurricanes ago, however, the shoreline eroded almost to the road, causing it to be officially closed to through-traffic from just past Sabine Pass to High Island on the southeast end. It is possible to drive this section of coast using the closed road and the beach with a four-wheel-drive or other heavy-duty vehicle, and some excellent surf fishing is found within this area, but most visitors would be better served beginning their trip down the Texas beach at High Island. In fact this site is so spectacular that I've included it among the Special Places—see that chapter toward the end of the book.

1 Rollover Pass

Rollover Pass is a narrow portion of the peninsula where it is said that during Prohibition days, rum smugglers would land their barrels of illegal booze in the surf from small boats launched from larger vessels anchored a bit offshore. The barrels were then "rolled over" to other boats waiting on the shore of East Bay, thus avoiding the need to dock in a port where scrutiny of the cargo would be much greater.

A sportsmen's group from the Beaumont–Port Arthur area obtained funding and permission from the state to cut a channel joining bay and Gulf to provide a means for fish to traverse between the two bodies of water, and fishing for speckled trout and flounder is often excellent here. Anglers line the banks of the "pass" shoulder to shoulder when flounder are running—usually fall and again in the spring—and during the annual late fall run of "golden" croakers. Surf fishing in front of the pass is good for reds and trout, but waders should always be wary of strong currents too near any pass from bay to Gulf, especially during tidal changes.

Several incorporated communities are located along Highway 87 on Bolivar Peninsula, and all offer bait camps, accommodations, food, and fuel. There are also many beachfront homes, though most are vacation homes used more in the summer months. By state law, the beach in front of these homes is open to anglers and casual beachgoers alike. RV parks are also in the area, including one right at Rollover Pass.

2 Bolivar Pocket

The surf can be fished all the way to the North Galveston Jetty, one of the two massive granite jetties that protect the Galveston entrance from the Gulf. There is a small boat cut through the jetty almost at the beach, which allows boaters to access what is known as the "Bolivar Pocket," where the beach butts up against the jetty.

Rollover Pass, Bolivar Pocket, Galveston Island, San Luis Pass

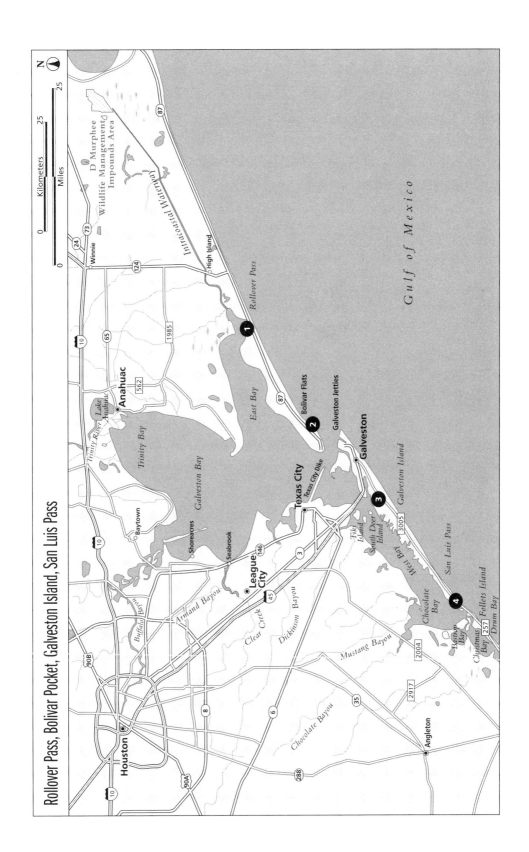

Fishing here can be excellent, especially when the winds leave the pocket protected and calm. One thing to remember when wading here is that anglers who love to tangle with really big stingrays on rod and reel consider the pocket a prime hunting ground! This area can be great for anything from panfish and speckled trout to bull reds and large sharks, depending mostly on the tackle and techniques employed. Like most of the upper coast surf, warm weather—spring through fall—is the key to good fishing.

3 Galveston Island

Galveston is the tourist center of the northeastern Texas coast, and it is filled with history from pirate and Indian days. The first barrier island on the Texas coast to be encountered when traveling east to west, Galveston is reached from the Bolivar Peninsula by a car ferry running across "Bolivar Roads"—the intersection of the ICW, the Galveston Ship Channel heading offshore, and Galveston Bay. The only other means of getting on the island by vehicle are the causeway bridge carrying Interstate 45 (which links Houston and Galveston) across the bay, and the point where Follets Island is exited, over the San Luis Pass Toll Bridge at the extreme western end of the island.

Galveston has hotels, restaurants, shell shops, and nightlife in abundance for visitors, as well as all the facilities to be expected from one of the state's largest cities. It also has a rich fishing tradition and offers opportunities aplenty for shore-bound anglers. State Highway 3005 runs the length of the island along the seawall—a barrier built when the entire island was razed after the 1900 hurricane devastated the

The Galveston surf pounds the shore with the 61st Street Pier in the background.

city. Along the seawall are many rock groins, small granite jetties built to control the movement of currents and sand along the beach. These structures are used as free fishing piers by surf anglers wanting more distance from shore—and from the beach crowds.

There are also two excellent commercial piers along the seawall: the 61st Street Pier, at the intersection of Seawall Boulevard and 61st Street, and the Gulf Coast Pier farther down the seawall. Both offer shots at everything from panfish to king mackerel and tarpon, in season. Spring through fall is best for warm-weather species, but panfish like croaker, whiting, and sometimes pompano are taken in winter. In fact, a state record tarpon of over 210 pounds was taken off the Gulf Coast pier, a Galveston pier in late 2006. A fishing pier is also located at the Flagship Hotel, which itself is built on a huge pier over the water.

Just past the point where the seawall ends is Galveston Island State Park, where camping facilities are available right off the beach. It is no longer permissible to drive the beach on most of the island, but selected parking areas are arranged close enough for anglers to easily walk to the surf. The advantage to this is that vehicular traffic on the beach often drives fish away. The park has been closed to beach driving longer than any other area on the island. Beach campfires have also been prohibited on the island for many years.

When I spent every weekend fishing the Galveston surf back in the mid to late 1970s, I would often drive the beach from just past the park all the way to San Luis Pass, sand conditions permitting. There were only a few beach subdivisions and small incorporated communities that ended long before reaching the pass. Those days are long gone, I'm afraid, and on the drive from the end of the seawall to the pass, it is now almost impossible to catch a glimpse of the water over the dunes because of all the massive "beach mansions" that have been built.

4 San Luis Pass

A large subdivision is going in at San Luis Pass, with plans for some sort of marina on the bay side. Fishing the beach is still legal and possible, but driving or parking on it are not, except at the pass itself—at least for now.

San Luis Pass allows water exchange between West Bay and the Gulf of Mexico. It is famous for its strong currents, which provide excellent fishing opportunities but are also very dangerous. Many, many people have drowned here during strong outgoing tides. It is advisable to fish from the bank and wade only at slack tides—and with a life jacket on. The pass is reached by driving through the city of Galveston proper down Seawall Boulevard, State Highway 3005, then continuing to the end of the island. The San Luis Pass toll bridge, which charges a $2 fee to cross, connects Galveston Island to Follets Island, crossing over San Luis Pass to do so. San Luis Pass is famous for speckled trout fishing, but also for larger species such as bull reds and jack crevalle. Tarpon are caught in the pass and just offshore, as well as large sharks. While most activity is in the warmer months, big black drum move through the pass in late February through early March, and panfish are present all year-round.

Follets Island to Sargent

---

5 Follets Island

This section of beach is much less developed than Galveston Island and offers more secluded fishing areas—though it can become crowded on warm holiday weekends. Crossing the San Luis Pass Toll Bridge from West Galveston Island puts you on Follets Island, which really isn't an island anymore. The San Luis Pass Fishing Pier is immediately off the bridge, and there is a county park on the north side of the road—designated County Road 257 at this point, or the Bluewater Highway—that offers camping, a boat ramp, and other amenities. The Bright Light Grocery also has bait and tackle.

Depending on sand conditions, the beach can be accessed here by automobile, and it is often possible to drive along the water all the way to the village of Surfside. As on the Bolivar Peninsula, there will be access cuts through the dunes at fairly regular intervals.

One of the most famous spots to fish on this stretch of beach is "The Boilers," the remains of a Confederate Civil War blockade-runner steamship whose boiler sections can be seen above the water on calm days and at low tide, just beyond the second sandbar. Several cars have been sunk in the sand near the pass over the years in an attempt to fight beach erosion, and they have also ended up providing near-shore fish-attracting structure in the surf. For the past few years, a large Gulf shrimp boat that was grounded with its bow facing out to sea has been a very easily located landmark that orients fish as well as anglers. These structures are very good at times in the spring and summer for speckled trout, either on live shrimp or Johnson Sprite spoons. The spoons come with a small red plastic tab at their base, above the hook, and replacement packages of these tabs are available. A wise surf angler will carry these extras, because the tabs come off during fast action with trout, and when this occurs, the lure is no longer as effective.

Bull redfish are possible most months and are probable from spring to late fall for long rodders, along with jack crevalles, sharks, rays, and smaller species. Black drums to very large sizes can be encountered in the pass and sometimes along the beach immediately outside the pass. Live blue crabs are the top bait for these bruisers.

6 Surfside

Some beach access for anglers is provided inside the Surfside city limits, and the Surfside Jetty is a popular spot. But some areas of the beach are off-limits to vehicles, and others require a city-issued permit. In warm weather, anglers can be seen wading the surf for speckled trout almost to the base of the jetty. The jetty park has restrooms and parking at a point where visitors can observe both the surf and the Gulf-bound vessels heading out through the jetties.

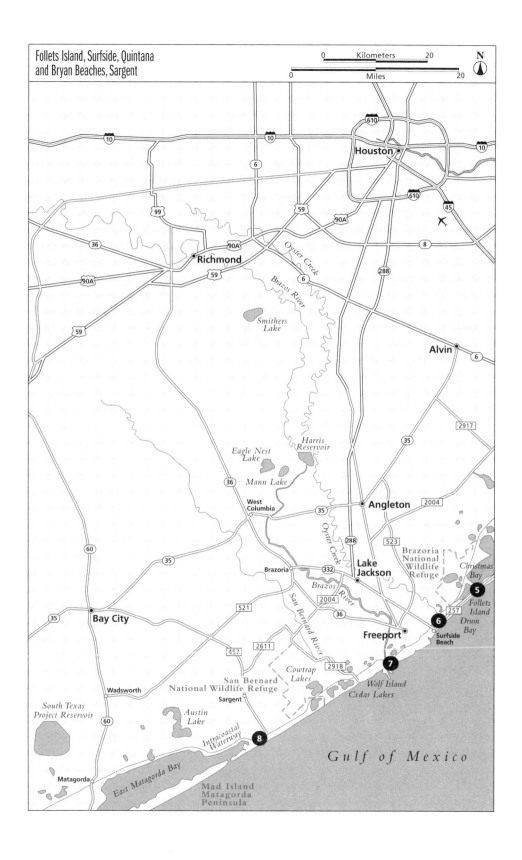

Follets Island, Surfside, Quintana
and Bryan Beaches, Sargent

Kilometers

Miles

N

Houston

Richmond

Alvin

Smithers
Lake

Brazos River

Oyster Creek

Harris
Reservoir

Eagle Nest
Lake

Mann Lake

West
Columbia

Angleton

Oyster Creek

Brazoria
National
Wildlife
Refuge

Christmas
Bay

Follets
Island

Drum
Bay

Brazoria

Lake
Jackson

Brazos River

San Bernard River

Bay City

Freeport

Surfside
Beach

Wadsworth

San Bernard
National Wildlife Refuge

Sargent

Cowtrap
Lakes

Wolf Island

Cedar Lakes

South Texas
Project Reservoir

Austin
Lake

Intracoastal
Waterway

Gulf of Mexico

Matagorda

East Matagorda Bay

Mad Island
Matagorda
Peninsula

5

6

7

8

Surfside beach and surf are viewed from the jetty.

Jetty species are trout, reds, flounder, and various panfish, plus bull reds, tarpon, Spanish and king mackerel at the end. Best fishing occurs in warmer weather for all but the big reds, who are more likely to visit in the fall.

To get to jetty park, take 332 (from the north) across the Surfside Bridge to the red light at the intersection with CR 257 coming from San Luis Pass. Turn right (or go straight in coming in on 257) on Velasco, then left when it ends at Parkview Road.

7 Quintana and Bryan Beaches

You need to drive to the very end of Highway 288 in Freeport to access the Quintana Jetty, Quintana Beach, and Bryan Beach, but no permit or fee is required on these beaches as of this writing. Bait and tackle are available in Freeport and in Quintana. Access to the area—which is, in effect, an island between the "Old" and "New" Brazos River outlets, the Gulf, and the ICW—has been much improved by replacing the old "swing" bridge across the ICW with a new high-span fixed structure.

Turn right where the road meets the beach, and you are heading down Bryan Beach. Unless the sand is very soft or the tide is very high, it is possible to drive the beach westward all the way to the mouth of the "New" Brazos River. As with anywhere on the Texas coast, a four-wheel-drive vehicle will make beach travel more certain. This arm of the river was created when the U.S. Army Corps of Engineers blocked off the lower section of the original river channel. This created Freeport Harbor and a jettied Gulf outlet for shipping interests related to the heavy concentration of petrochemical plants in the Brazosport area. The Corps also dug what is known by industry as the "diversion canal" and by nearly everyone else as the "new" Brazos River outlet. It is not always possible to drive from the end of the paved road on the beach back to the jetty, but it can be easily accessed by blacktop pavement through the village of Quintana. Bryan Beach, all the way to the river, is now within the city limits of Freeport and has been provided with portable toilets and trash cans along the way.

The farther from the pavement, and thus the closer to the river you can get, the smaller the beach crowds and the better the fishing opportunities. After Tropical Storm Claudette in 1979, when 44 inches of rain fell in this area in less than twenty-four hours, the beach was cut by several deep trenches washed out by storm tides and heavy runoff. Fishing close to one of these cuts in clear, green surf with long-rod tackle and live mullet for bait, I hooked and landed a 27-pound king mackerel from the beach, surprising many people driving along the sand.

A "delta" of shallow water formed by the river extends over 100 yards into the Gulf on the Bryan Beach side, and it can be a feeding ground for bull reds, jack crevalles, and speckled trout. It is also a spot frequented by some very large sharks and haunted by sometimes-dangerous currents, so waders here should be extra careful. In the mid-1970s, a state-record tiger shark of more than 700 pounds was taken from the beach here, hooked in a deep hole just to the east of the delta that is often worked by wade fishers after specks.

The river itself is a great spot for trout, reds of all sizes, flounder, and jacks. It is also one of the best spots on the upper coast for really big gafftop catfish. At one time the Brazos was famous for tarpon fishing, and these silver gamesters can still be found a little upriver at a chemical plant's warm-water outlet. The Brazos can be very good for speckled trout in winter when a cold front has dropped temperatures to freezing or below and the water is exceptionally clear. Migratory species like jack crevalles and tarpon are best in warm weather months, flounder in spring. I have seen bull reds caught at the mouth in January, but fall is a more predictable time for the big reds. Speckled trout roam the surf near the river mouth all summer, as do large shark.

8 Sargent

To reach the beach on either side of Sargent, take FM 457 east, which intersects FM 521 at Cedar Lane. Bait and tackle are available in Sargent, as well as two nice restaurants. Caney Creek enters the Gulf here, crossing the beach at a cut spanned by a bridge leading to the beach east of Sargent.

Several years ago the U.S. Army Corps of Engineers dug a cut from the ICW to the Gulf just west of Sargent to allow shrimp boats access to Gulf waters. This was in response to a lawsuit by shrimp boat operators because the Corps had dredged a section of the ICW and pumped the spoil into East Matagorda Bay, silting it up and ruining shrimping there for the season. Some local businessmen thought it would be good to have a deeper cut, so they enlisted a large tugboat to "wash" the channel with its props. Several coastal storms later, the beach at Sargent had washed away so severely that the ICW would soon be running across a section of open Gulf. The

Corps rebuilt the land between the Gulf and ICW, at the same time creating a large paved parking lot on the canal side, with picnic areas and restrooms. The cut to the Gulf is still there, blocking vehicular traffic onto Matagorda Peninsula from Sargent, but it is much smaller and the banks are supported against further erosion.

The surf at Sargent gets less fishing pressure than areas to the northeast, as it is farther from major population centers and the permanent and weekend residents concentrate largely on fishing in Caney Creek or East Matagorda Bay. Speckled trout are present in Caney Creek from spring through fall, with some action possible in winter months. "Rat" reds run the creek in large numbers in the fall. The surf is good for both species plus panfish species from spring through late fall.

Matagorda Peninsula to Mustang Island

9 Matagorda Peninsula

The Matagorda Peninsula functions much like a barrier island between the Gulf and East Matagorda Bay, and it is actually only barely a peninsula and not an island. Separated from the mainland at Sargent by the cut described in site 10, it can only be reached by vehicle near the mouth of the Colorado River, many miles to the south. On the west side of the river, no vehicle access is possible on the portion of the peninsula from the river mouth to the jettied pass across the bay from Port O'Connor.

So, to reach the eastern end of the peninsula, you must drive to the river mouth first. From Sargent, take FM 457 back to FM 521 and drive west to the small town of Wadsworth, where you take Highway 60 south. An alternate route is Highway 35 west to Bay City, then south on Highway 60. Crossing the ICW to the beach requires using a swing bridge at the historic small town of Matagorda, and delays are caused when the bridge opens for traffic coming down the canal. This bridge is scheduled for replacement by a new fixed span bridge within the next few years. There is a new marina at Matagorda, with a bait camp, boat ramp, fuel, and a nice restaurant, plus bait, supplies, food, and lodging are available in the town. Highway 60 ends at Matagorda, so take FM 2031 the final 7 miles to the river mouth. There are more bait camps and facilities along the river on your way.

A two-wheel-drive vehicle can make a good portion of the trip east on the peninsula in favorable conditions, but four-wheel drive is necessary to safely travel all the way to the cut across from Sargent. Once away from the river mouth area, which has a jettied entrance with the east jetty functioning as a free fishing pier (note that this area suffered extensive storm damage in 2005, but rebuilding efforts are under way), the peninsula is undeveloped land, giving anglers on foot both bay- and surf-fishing opportunities. When walking through the saltgrass of the dunes, however, always be sure to watch for rattlesnakes! Other wildlife commonly encountered include coyotes, raccoons, birds of prey such as ospreys, and an occasional white-tailed deer.

In the "old days," Brown Cedar Cut was the point of no return for drivers heading east on the beach, and it provided legendary fishing on both the bay and surf sides because of the currents washing through. Brown Cedar has been sanded closed for many years now, but still marks an excellent and usually secluded fishing spot. It is possible along this beach, especially during midweek and in the fall, to reach a point where you can look to the horizon in both directions and not see a single car or man-made structure. The water just off the beach is deeper here than off beaches to the east, especially as you travel closer to Brown Cedar, so larger fish such as bull reds and sharks may feed almost to the sand, and long casts are not

Matagorda Peninsula, Matagorda Island

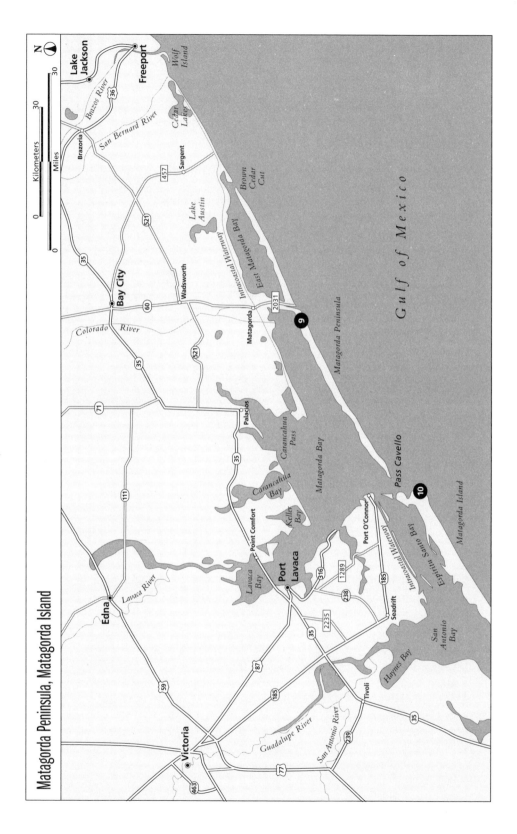

N

Kilometers
0   30
0   30
Miles

Lake Jackson

Freeport

Brazos River

36

Brazoria

San Bernard River

457

Sargent

Cedar Lakes

Wolf Island

Lake Austin

521

Wadsworth

Intracoastal Waterway

Brown Cedar Cut

East Matagorda Bay

35

Bay City

60

Colorado River

521

Matagorda

2031

9

Matagorda Peninsula

Gulf of Mexico

71

Palacios

35

Carancahua Pass

Carancahua Bay

Matagorda Bay

Point Comfort

Keller Bay

111

Port Comfort

Lavaca Bay

Pass Cavello

10

Matagorda Island

316

1289

Port O'Connor

Edna

Lavaca River

Port Lavaca

238

185

Intracoastal Waterway

Espíritu Santo Bay

2235

35

Seadrift

87

59

Victoria

185

Guadalupe River

San Antonio River

Haynes Bay

San Antonio Bay

Tivoli

239

35

463

77

necessary to reach them with a baited hook. Flounder are also common along the shoreline, and I have even found them trapped in tidal pools, where I could "gig" them with a fillet knife.

For anglers seeking a remote spot to camp and fish that can be reached fairly easily by vehicle, this portion of the Texas coast is a great choice. The "peninsula" on the other side of the Colorado River also offers excellent fishing but in a much more remote setting, requiring a boat to get there along with all the precautions advised for such locations. Fall is my favorite time for this stretch of beach, as the fishing is great, the weather cooler, and the crowds much thinner—but good fishing can be found from spring through the warmer months.

10 Matagorda Island

The island called Matagorda begins on the western side of the Gulf pass opposite the small fishing village of Port O'Connor and is quickly cut by Pass Cavalla, a shallow passage offering great fishing for various species from trout to tarpon, but only for those with boats. Port O'Connor is reached by leaving Highway 35—the paved artery that replaces Highway 87 along this section of the coast as the favored route—at Port Lavaca and taking FM 238 west to FM 185, or continuing west out of Port Lavaca on Highway 35 to its intersection with FM 185. Port O'Connor itself is a fishing and offshore oil-field community, but property here is highly sought after by inland residents for weekend and retirement homes due to the excellent fishing and waterfowl hunting.

Matagorda Island was once the site of a military base, and some buildings and the remains of an airstrip still exist. The property is now a state park, so the landing of private planes is no longer allowed, but there are facilities for day visitors and limited camping. Ferry service to the island is provided by the state from Port O'Connor, also on a limited basis. Port O'Connor is famous for speckled trout in spring through fall, and for large numbers of flounder taken by giggers in the fall. Tarpon are common in Pass Cavallo in late summer and early fall. Redfish love the jetties and roam the back bay grasses in fall.

11 San Jose Island

Across another cut, Matagorda Island becomes San Jose Island. The "jetty boat" runs from Port Aransas to San Jose's several times each day to take sightseers, bird watchers, and fishers to the island, with most anglers opting to fish the east Port Aransas jetty. Port Aransas is on Mustang Island off Highway 35, a ferry ride across Redfish Bay from the Rockport/Fulton communities. While warmer months are prime along the whole coast, this area begins the portion of the state that has normally warmer waters and sees an annual influx of "winter" Texans. Fishing is a favorite activity of these visitors, who are often as pleased with panfish as with speckled trout. Trout, redfish, and flounder may be caught year-round in this area, where the temperatures average milder than on the upper coast and the water is clearer.

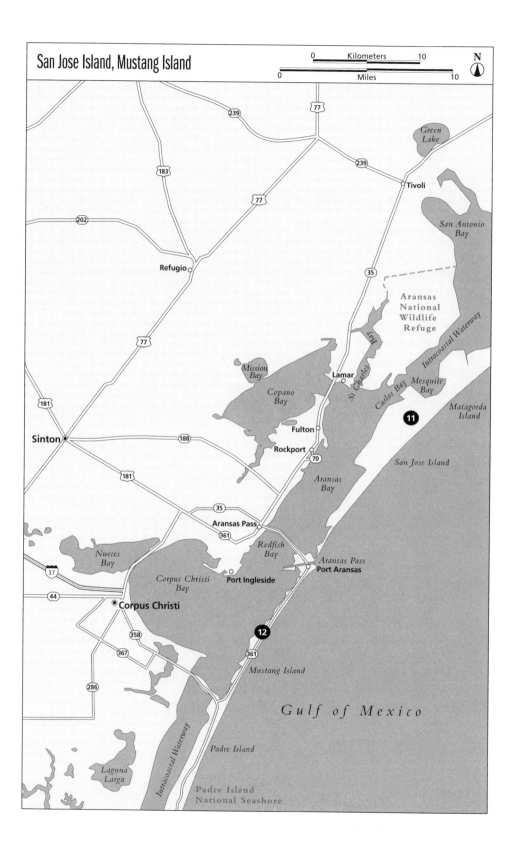

San Jose Island, Mustang Island

0 Kilometers 10
0 Miles 10

N

Green Lake

239

77

239

Tivoli

183

77

San Antonio Bay

202

35

Refugio

Aransas National Wildlife Refuge

Intracoastal Waterway

77

Mission Bay

Lamar

St. Charles Bay

Carlos Bay

Mesquite Bay

Copano Bay

11

Matagorda Island

181

Fulton

San Jose Island

Sinton

188

Rockport

70

181

Aransas Bay

35

Aransas Pass

361

Redfish Bay

Aransas Pass

Port Aransas

Nueces Bay

37

Corpus Christi Bay

Port Ingleside

44

Corpus Christi

358

12

367

361

Mustang Island

286

Gulf of Mexico

Intracoastal Waterway

Padre Island

Laguna Larga

Padre Island National Seashore

12 Mustang Island

Mustang Island is more developed than the coastal areas between it and Galveston, but it still has opportunities for surf anglers. The south jetty at Port Aransas is a good route to deep water on foot. Driving-on-the-beach opportunities are sadly limited here, although the wide stretch of sand on Mustang is comparable to Daytona Beach for being packed and easily traveled.

Highway 361 leaves Highway 35 at Aransas Pass and crosses Redfish Bay and the pass itself (via the ferry) to Port Aransas at the north end of Mustang Island. Hwy 361 then runs all the way to North Padre Island, where it is supplanted by Park Road 22. There are access points to the surf between Port Aransas and Padre Island, and Packery Channel to the Gulf has recently been reopened as a fish pass.

Port Aransas offers a resort atmosphere as well as being a fishing destination, and surf fishing is an ingrained tradition here. The jetties have long been popular with shark fishers, of which there is an active community. Water clarity in the surf is normally much better on this portion of the coast than around Galveston or High Island because no major rivers have outlets to the Gulf from roughly the Colorado to the Rio Grande, leaving the sand much whiter with less river mud mixed in.

This section of the coast is often referred to as the "Texas Riviera" for the beauty of its beaches and the water. At Mustang Island, we see the civilized edge of the Texas surf angler's mecca—Padre Island.

The species and seasons are roughly the same as nearby areas—speckled trout through panfish year-round, tarpon and other migratory species mostly in warmer months.

The Islands of the Padre and the Mouth of the Rio Grande

Padre Island was so-named because it was once deeded to a Spanish priest, when Texas was under the rule of Spain. The two sections of the Padre make up the longest barrier island on the Gulf coast and protect the Laguna Madre—the most unique bay system on any U.S. coast.

13 North Padre Island

Across a nondescript bridge from Mustang Island is North Padre, a 70-plus-mile run of largely undeveloped beach, much of it accessible only by four-wheel drive—and even then, not all the time. If coming from Corpus Christi, take Highway 358 to the island over the causeway bridge. Most of North Padre is in the Padre Island National Seashore. Park Road 22 runs a short distance down the island; the beach is the only road from its end to the Mansfield Cut. A fee is charged to enter the national seashore, and permits are required for overnight stays. Permits can be obtained at the entrance gate.

Just before the park is an island institution—the famous Bob Hall fishing pier. Over the years, countless huge sharks and big tarpon have been caught off this pier, though shark fishing is discouraged in these modern times to avoid frightening beachgoers. The Bob Hall pier is still an excellent fishing spot and easily reached by any type of vehicle.

Once inside the national seashore and off the pavement, a lot of open beach beckons the angler. Two of the more famous spots are known as Big Shell and Little Shell. Little Shell is first, and it can sometimes be reached with a two-wheel-drive pickup or SUV. In this area tiny coquina shells have washed ashore, probably over centuries, and they clearly mark a bed of these shellfish past the breakers that attract all kinds of feeding game fish. They also make for a very soft, deep bed of shell that sucks at vehicle tires, making a serious four-wheel drive necessary to travel much farther. Big Shell is similarly composed, but of larger shells washed ashore, and it also marks a traditionally excellent fishing area.

Shark fishers from all over the state have journeyed down the beach to Big and Little Shell for decades to run baits out for monsters, often having elevated platforms on their vehicles to keep their lines out of the crashing surf and above what little traffic might come down the beach at night. The availability and popularity of four-wheel-drive vehicles has meant an increase of such traffic, but the far reaches of North Padre Island are still not places one gets to "just passing through."

The end of the line is the Mansfield Cut, a jettied pass across the Laguna Madre from Port Mansfield, which allows access to the Gulf for recreational anglers, shrimp boats, and oil-field supply boats. The channel is sanded in quite a bit as of this writing, with a depth of only 5 feet in some spots at low tide, but efforts are

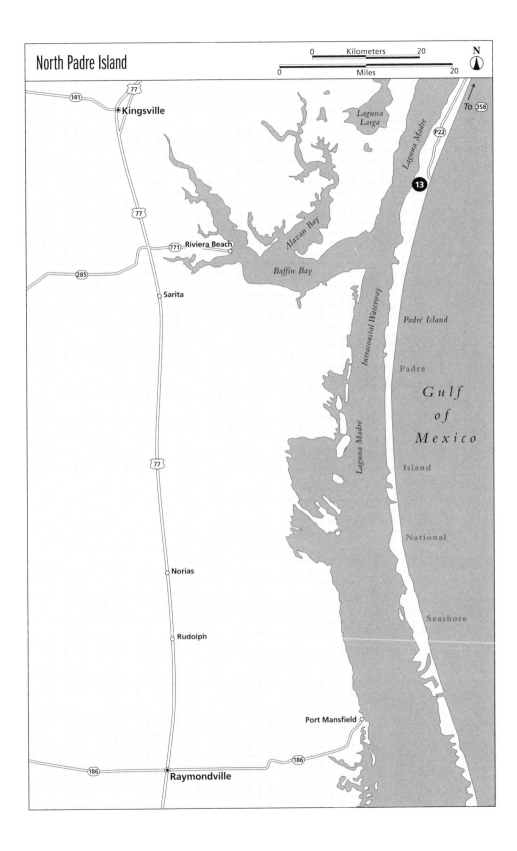

North Padre Island

0   Kilometers   20

0   Miles   20

N

141

77   Kingsville

To 358

Laguna Larga

Laguna Madre

P22

13

77

771   Riviera Beach

Alazan Bay

285

Baffin Bay

Sarita

Padre Island

Intracoastal Waterway

Padre

Gulf
of
Mexico

Laguna Madre

Island

77

National

Norias

Seashore

Rudolph

Port Mansfield

186

186   Raymondville

under way to get it dredged. If you can make it to the cut, great fishing opportunities await. The surf is excellent for any of the usual species found off Texas beaches, and the shallow Laguna Madre behind the island offers excellent wade fishing. The jetties are not especially long, but they attract and hold tarpon, king mackerel, and other glamour species in warm weather. An extra bonus here is the real possibility of hooking a snook in either the surf or the bay. These mostly tropical fish have increased in number enough along this part of the coast that some guides specialize in taking clients out for them.

Anyone venturing this far down Padre Island should bring anything they might need with them, as there are no stores, bait camps, motels, or gas stations to be found. Emergency food and water, fuel, and first-aid equipment are very important, as are a spare tire, oil, and coolant for vehicles. An extra starting battery is also a good idea. Shovels for digging out of soft sand are standard equipment, and a vehicle-mounted winch is a plus. Padre will test your and your equipment's mettle, but it can be an unforgettable experience. There are a few guides who take anglers "down island" for surf fishing, which might be a good way for visitors to get a taste of what this part of the coast can offer.

14 South Padre Island

South Padre is truly "Texas Tropic," with a climate similar to south Florida. The beach is white and beautiful, the water clear and green. While South Padre can be seen from the north side of the Mansfield Cut, you can't get there by vehicle. You must drive back to Corpus Christi and take U.S. Highway 77 (the pathway to south Texas after Corpus) south either to Los Fresnos and then go east 26 miles on FM 100 to Port Isabel, or to Brownsville and head east for 24 miles on FM 48 to Port Isabel. Port Isabel is on the mainland just across from South Padre Island, where the causeway to the island itself begins. South Padre is a prime vacation retreat. Caution should be used whenever planning trips to the Texas coast in early spring but especially down here, due to the huge number of college students on "spring break" who come to party and enjoy the beaches.

For anglers, the fun starts on the north jetty, which protects the Brownsville Ship Channel. All kinds of exotic fish may be encountered here, including snook and tarpon, and king mackerel are caught by rock walkers, usually in the spring. Port Isabel and the City of South Padre Island offer all the amenities expected at a seashore resort, and there are guides to help visitors find fish. In addition, local tackle shops are happy to share information on where and how to catch various species.

The Mansfield Cut is much easier to reach from the south, if only because the distance from Port Isabel is about 35 miles. Park Road 100 runs north on the island for a short distance, then the beach becomes the highway. Because it is more accessible, South Padre may be a bit more crowded than the far reaches of North Padre, but it is still considered a remote area, where proper preparation and precautions can yield the trip of a lifetime for a surf angler.

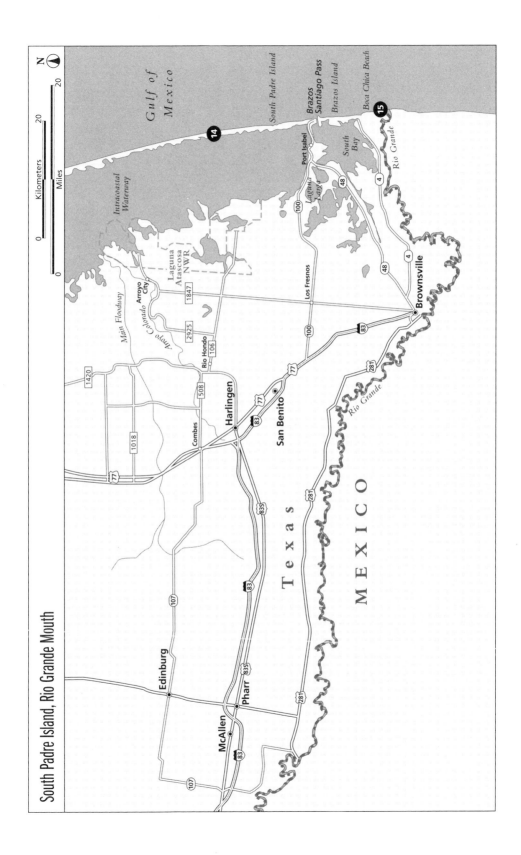

South Padre Island, Rio Grande Mouth

15 Rio Grande Mouth

The mouth of the Rio Grande is roughly 5 miles south of where FM 4 meets the beach. The river has suffered much from the impounding of two major lakes on its upper reaches and water diverted for irrigation throughout the fabled citrus-growing area of the Rio Grande Valley, and it will often be virtually dried up at the mouth in an especially hot and dry summer. Although it might be possible to walk or wade to the Mexican side, this is obviously not advisable.

Shark fishers after the big boys here will either swim their baits out or use some type of boat, whereas on the jetty it might be possible to float baits out with the tide. The only fatal shark attack ever recorded in Texas happened here, when a wade fisherman was cut in half by a big animal.

There is something really special about any river mouth, but even more so one that marks an international boundary. Standing on the north bank of the Rio Grande allows a look into the even more fabled fishing waters to the south. Besides big sharks, bull reds, speckled trout, and even tarpon and snook are possible here. Mild winter temperatures draw anglers from cooler areas on the north Texas coast, although spring and fall are probably better for fishing. Summers this far south can be very hot and humid, and anglers will find the beaches often crowded with sun-seekers.

At the mouth of the Rio Grande River, there are more anglers on the Mexican side. Those hills in the background are sand dunes!

Rivers and Passes

One of the best places on any coast to intercept fish is a pass between inshore bays or freshwater streams and the main body of salt water. On the Texas Gulf coast, this means river or creek outlets and the passes between bays and the Gulf. There are sixteen major streams that terminate in a bay or the Gulf itself, plus ten other passes. All of these outlets have some value as fishing spots, although some river mouths that are in bays are difficult to reach and fish, and a couple of the passes can only be reached by boat.

Most of the rivers, and many smaller streams, have a "saltwater barrier" upstream to keep salt water on high tides from intruding into irrigation canals and pumping stations. These are "low-water" dams that will allow high water to flow downstream. Since salt water is heavier than fresh, it will be on the bottom of the stream, as will saltwater fish. The same fish species, with some variation for temperate zones and bay-versus-Gulf species, will be found in most of these spots, and thus similar tackle and techniques are appropriate.

For our purposes, we will again begin at the Louisiana border and discuss each spot in the order we come to it.

16 Sabine River, Neches River, and Sabine Pass

Both the Sabine River and the Neches River end in Sabine Lake, a small, shallow bay on the state border. The Sabine actually enters as the Sabine-Neches Canal, though there is an outlet combining part of the river with Black Bayou on the Louisiana side of the lake. The Neches terminates in the same canal on the edge of the lake, in an industrial area. Neither of these spots is a vital fishery, but a run upriver on an incoming tide can produce some species of saltwater fish, especially flounder and redfish. Sabine Lake is probably a better option, however, for those with a boat.

Sabine Pass was originally the natural outlet of Sabine Lake, but is now the point where the Port Arthur Ship Channel enters the Gulf. The pass itself is jettied, but it can only be reached by boat. Highway 87, which used to lead south to High Island, has been closed by storm damage. Now it ends at Sabine Pass Battleground Park, where there is a boat ramp and bank-fishing possibilities. The jetties are good for speckled trout, redfish, and flounder, as well as a variety of panfish. Although fish can be taken all year, because this is the most northern pass on the Texas coast, warmer weather pays off in better fishing action for reds and trout. Flounder and big black drum also use the pass for migration to the Gulf.

17 Trinity River and Rollover Pass

The Trinity River feeds Trinity Bay, a very productive body of water that is part of the Galveston Bay system. Upstream on the Trinity is Lake Livingston, a large freshwater impoundment popular with anglers all over the state. Partly because of the lake, and partly because this area gets a lot of rain, the Trinity is subject to frequent flooding, which often leaves the lower reaches of the river and the bay itself muddy and full of freshwater. When the river is low and high tides can push upstream, speckled trout may be caught as far as the Interstate 10 bridge, which is

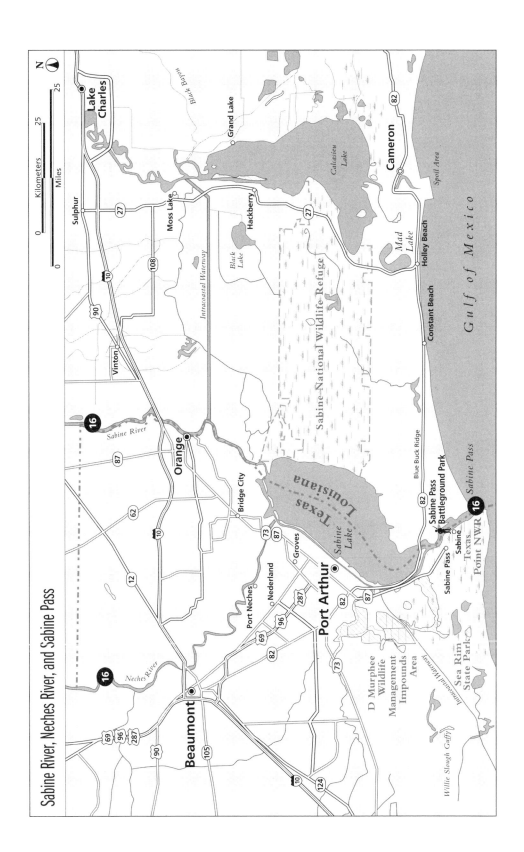

Sabine River, Neches River, and Sabine Pass

Trinity River and Rollover Pass, Galveston Area

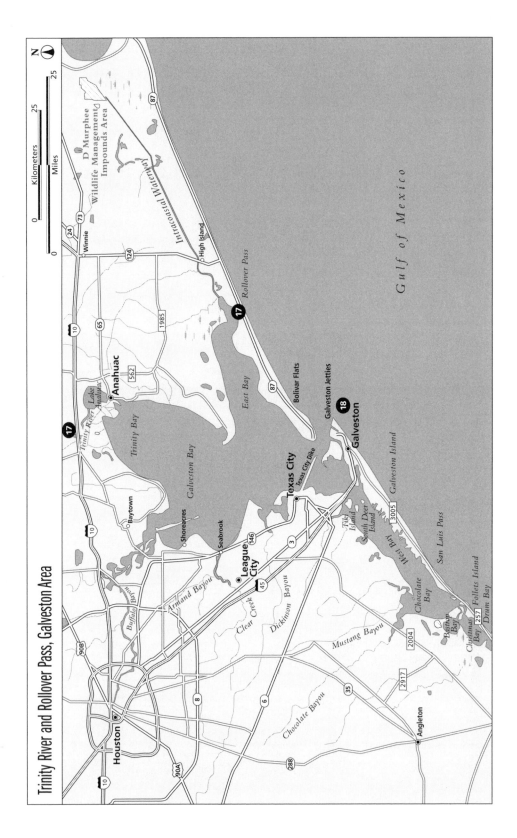

as good a place as any for bank anglers to work the river, as it is only a few miles upstream from where the river ends in the bay.

The actual juncture of the river with the bay is similar to the situation at the mouth of the Mississippi River, with many small streams and passes branching off and entering the bay. Most of these are shallow and relatively insignificant, and the area is swampy. The main outlet is the Anahuac Channel, which enters the bay at the town of Anahuac. Fort Anahuac Park is near the channel, and it is a good spot for bank anglers and also has a boat ramp. Anahuac is reached most easily from I-10 by taking Highway 124 south through Winnie, then going east on Highway 65.

The Old River, which is an arm of the Trinity cut off by a course change years ago, also terminates in Trinity Bay, very near the outlet of the Trinity River. The Old River is very shallow, at least where it crosses under I-10, which makes it an excellent flounder area. When I was in junior high school, I remember hundreds of people gathering between the Old and Trinity Rivers during flood periods to seine for crawfish, the delectable "ditch bugs" beloved here and in Louisiana as a sort of very small lobster.

Rollover Pass is discussed in the surf-fishing section of this book, but it is worthy of another mention. As one of the few man-made passes constructed solely as a "fish pass," it is fairly unusual. While it has been a boon to anglers, providing easy access to anyone who can drive up on Highway 87, it has been blamed for beach erosion on the Gulf side and sanding in on the bay side. As is often the case, although the fishing has been great, nature has shown us why she didn't put a pass there in the first place! Rollover is famous for runs of "golden croaker" in the fall; it also hosts runs of flounder going into the Gulf in the fall and returning in spring. Speckled trout action both in the Gulf surf and in the bay inside the pass is good from spring through late fall. Some sort of panfish will likely be found feeding through in any month of the year.

18 Galveston Area

Galveston, being a true island, naturally has a pass on both ends. On the eastern end, the Houston Ship Channel enters the Gulf by crossing Bolivar Roads and passing through the longest set of jetties on the Gulf coast. The Galveston jetties are also spaced farther apart than any others. Fishing opportunities begin at the ferry landing on the Bolivar side, where there are rock groins that anglers can use extending toward the depths of the channel. There is also a pier reaching out into the channel. Both jetties can be walked, although the small boat cut on the "north" jetty limits how far rock walkers can go.

Boaters will find tremendous opportunities around the jetties, as well as a short distance offshore. Inside the "south" jetty are sandbars that can be waded and a shallow area known as Fleenor Flats, which is famous for schooling bull reds in the fall. Speckled trout fishing is excellent around the jetties when rains have sweetened the bays with freshwater. Redfish, sheepshead, black drum, and flounder are also common along the jetties. There is a deep hole off the end of the south jetty where several state record tiger sharks have been captured, and in this same area in the 1950s, the still-current state record jewfish (Goliath grouper) and sawfish were caught. Winter fishing in the relatively deep water along the jetties pays off in speckled trout, and the same is true anytime heavy rains have caused freshwater run off from the Trinity River to push trout to the comfortable salinity of the Gulf. Bull reds feed on Fleenor Flats best in the fall, and pelagic species like Spanish mackerel, tarpon, big shark, and the occasional king mackerel will be warm-weather visitors, from spring through a mild late fall.

Back on the mainland side of Galveston Bay, the **San Jacinto River** ends in a juncture with the Houston Ship Channel. The San Jacinto is popular with water-skiers and offers excellent freshwater fishing farther upstream, and the tidal portion is "coming back" after decades of heavy industrial pollution. Although black bass and crappie are present, more anglers probably seek big catfish here, of all the larger freshwater species. Fishing is best in spring and fall.

On the island itself, **Offatts Bayou** wanders from almost the middle of the island to West Bay. Offatts is very deep in spots, making it a popular anchorage for visiting boaters, both sail and power. It is also one of the very best winter fishing spots in the area for speckled trout. Trout gather in warmer, deeper water when cold temperatures force them out of the shallower portions of the bays. While lures and live and dead bait all work on these chilled fish, they feed much more sluggishly in cold water, so work the lure slowly and be patient with bait. Offatts can be reached from 61st Street, where baits camps and boat ramps are located, or by water off West Bay and the Intracoastal Waterway (ICW).

On the west end of Galveston Island is **San Luis Pass**, the natural outlet of West Bay to the Gulf. San Luis Pass is famous for both excellent wade fishing and for drownings. The currents on an outgoing tide can be very strong, and the bottom can fall away quickly. Bank fishing for trout, reds, and flounder is excellent on both sides of the pass, both bay and Gulf. In the spring, swarms of Spanish mackerel may enter the pass from the Gulf, and both big sharks and jack crevalles can be caught in the pass and in the surf on both sides.

The Galveston side of the pass currently is being built up as an upscale housing development, and beach access may be limited in the future. There are no bait camps or boat ramps near the pass on the east side, but several communities toward the city of Galveston have facilities on the bay side. The west side of the pass has the Bright Light Grocery, grocery/bait store; the San Luis Pass Fishing Pier; and a Brazoria County park with a boat ramp, store, and RV parking. There are spots in the park along the bank fronting the deep channel coming from the pass that are excellent for big black drum in late March.

Water depth can be close to 20 feet where the channel runs under the bridge, and on a clear tide the bottom may be visible. This is a documented big-trout spot in spring and good for many species year-round. The pass pier has produced tarpon, lings, and big sharks in abundance over the years, and it is almost always good in warm weather for trout and reds. Storms change the pass each time one roars through, and even minor weather changes can have an effect. Where once the fishing pier extended to the channel running to the Gulf, Hurricane Alicia in 1983 sanded in that side of the pass and cut a new channel to the east. The beach near the pier has been steadily "moving" back to the area in front of the county park, which once was on the edge of the channel and offered drum fishing off a rip-rap bulkhead.

It is possible to get into West Bay from San Luis Pass, but because there are numerous sandbars and few channels, newcomers should be wary. On the other side of the bridge, since Hurricane Alicia in the early 1980s, the channel to deep water can be found due east from the bridge. On either side is very shallow water, and even when following the channel there is a large, shallow bar offshore of the pass that can be challenging. Despite all the possible dangers, however, San Luis Pass is one of the most consistent and easily accessible fishing hot spots on the upper Texas coast.

On the north side of West Bay, **Chocolate Bayou** widens into Chocolate Bay and joins West Bay at the ICW. Bayous are either tidal or rainwater streams, not fed by springs or lakes like rivers. The variety of marine life in the bayous is amazing, as the same stretch of water might yield trout, redfish, and flounder on a salty high tide, and black bass, crappie, and freshwater catfish on a fresher low tide. On average, much of Chocolate could be considered brackish—containing more salt water than freshwater, but less salt water than the bays or Gulf.

I lived on Chocolate in the small community of Liverpool for twenty-five years and caught blue, yellow, and channel catfish on trotlines; bass and reds on lures; and some huge alligator gars on both trotline and rod and reel. I also saw "baby" tarpon chasing bait past my dock on many occasions, indicating there may be a spawning population of tarpon in Texas water that scientists don't know about.

Lower Chocolate Bayou is reached from Highway 35, south on FM 203 to the community of Amsterdam, where Lutes Marina and Horseshoe Bend Marina have bait and launching facilities. Lutes has a heavy-duty lift, so trailers need not be backed into the water, and it also has gasoline. There is also a state boat ramp at the bridge on FM 2004, reached either by FM 203 or FM 2917 from Highway 35. Fishing in the bayou can be good at any time of the year, and it is more critical to watch the clarity of the water due to rains. Generally, fall will see clear, tidal water pushing in from the bay that jump-starts good fishing, while low winter tides leave a shallow, muddy stream in many stretches. Deeper holes might hold good fish in winter, if the rains have held off.

Bastrop Bayou would join West Bay around Coal Pass, but the ICW cuts it off below Christmas Bay. The bayou actually widens into Bastrop Bay across the ICW. This is an excellent area for reds and flounder, and it's not bad for trout. FM 227 off FM 2004 leads to a couple of small marinas with ramps, lifts, and bait on Bastrop, near the community of Demi-John and Demi-John Island. Bastrop is best for reds and flounder in the fall and spring and, like Chocolate Bayou, pays off when rains have not filled it with muddy freshwater runoff.

Oyster Creek flows into the ICW just before Freeport. Deep enough for large sportfishing boats to travel to the two marinas and several canal subdivisions upstream but bordered by the oyster reefs that give it its name, this creek has good fishing for reds, trout, and flounder. There is a public boat ramp in the city of Oyster Creek, and bank fishing is possible along the storm levee that protects the Brazosport area from storm surges and runs along the west bank of the creek for several miles.

Winter is probably the best time period for this body of water, as school-size speckled trout will come to feed under lights around docks and in the marinas. Redfish can be found feeding around grass beds and over oyster reefs in the main creek. Fishing in cooler weather when there is less boating traffic is also better.

19 Brazos River, San Bernard River, and Caney Creek

Long ago, in a galaxy not so far away, the Brazos River was diverted by the U.S. Army Corps of Engineers to form the "Old" Brazos, which is now the Freeport Harbor and enters the Gulf through the Freeport jetties. The Surfside Jetty is on the north and is paved with a flat surface almost to the end. The Quintana Jetty on the south side is also paved but lacks the railing the Surfside Jetty has because of storm damage a few years ago. Both jetties, as might be expected, attract fish of several species. Generally, trout will be better on the Gulf side of the jetty, while reds, black drum, and migrating flounder will be better on the channel side. Because the channel side is deeper and both sides of the rocks are bait-holding structure, fishing can be good all year, but spring through fall is best. Both commercial and sportfishing boats use this channel to reach the Gulf.

The Surfside Jetty is reached by taking Highway 332 to Surfside, then turning right at the first traffic light, Ft. Velasco Boulevard. There is a county park at the jetty, with bait, showers, food, and camping. To reach the Quintana Jetty on the south side, take "old" Highway 288 through Freeport, cross the new bridge over the ICW, and turn left at the first paved road. Bait camps and an RV park are located on this side.

Jetty fishing on Freeport's surfside jetty.

FISHING THE TEXAS GULF COAST

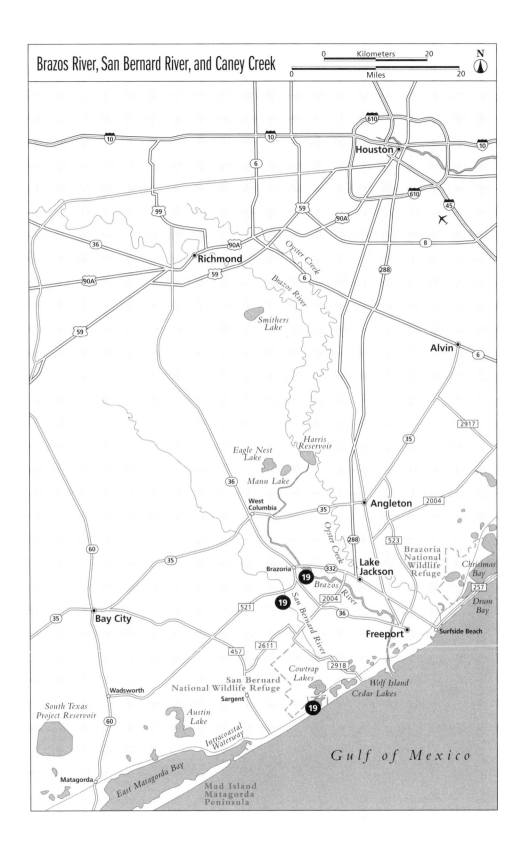

Brazos River, San Bernard River, and Caney Creek

Kilometers 0 — 20

Miles 0 — 20

N

Houston

Richmond

Alvin

Smithers Lake

Oyster Creek

Brazos River

Harris Reservoir

Eagle Nest Lake

Mann Lake

West Columbia

Angleton

Oyster Creek

Lake Jackson

Brazoria National Wildlife Refuge

Christmas Bay

Brazoria

Bay City

San Bernard River

Brazos River

Freeport

Surside Beach

Drum Bay

South Texas Project Reservoir

Wadsworth

Sargent

San Bernard National Wildlife Refuge

Austin Lake

Cowtrap Lakes

Wolf Island Cedar Lakes

Gulf of Mexico

Intracoastal Waterway

Matagorda

East Matagorda Bay

Mad Island Matagorda Peninsula

Drive to the beach and turn right (west) to reach the mouth of the "New" Brazos River.

The "New" Brazos runs into the Gulf to the west of Freeport and is reached on the east side by driving down the beach on Quintana and Bryan Beaches. The west side is an island formed by the Brazos and San Bernard Rivers and the ICW, and can only be reached by boat. The "New" Brazos is excellent for reds, both small keeper fish and the larger "bull" reds. Flounder are also a common catch, as are trout. At one time the Brazos was a famous tarpon spot, and the silver kings are still caught in the river. Jack crevalles enter the river mouth, as do bull sharks. In the winter the Brazos is excellent for speckled trout during periods of low rainfall, when the river is salty and clear. Tarpon are also caught upstream from the ICW crossing.

Bryan Beach can be driven on, and the portion annexed by the city of Freeport has conveniently spaced trash cans and portable toilets although the city is currently considering de-annexing the beach and discontinuing these services. Camping on the beach is permitted, as well as campfires. Small boats can be launched from the river bank, and there are ramps upstream, the best of which is located at the new Highway 36 bridge. A lock where the ICW crosses keeps debris coming downriver from obstructing the channel, and boaters wishing to travel to the San Bernard River or points farther south will have to get the lock operator to open it. Winter can be good for speckled trout, fall for bull reds, summer for any of the warmer weather species.

The San Bernard is a smaller river than the Brazos, in both size and length. At the time of this writing, the mouth of the San Bernard is sanded completely closed. Residents and some scientists believe the sand came from the rerouting of the Brazos, but in a short amount of time the mouth went from being an outlet that shrimp boats and small offshore boats could use to a sandbar. The river channel, such as it is, ends over 110 yards from the Gulf. The U.S. Army Corps of Engineers has recently agreed to reopen the mouth, and dredging was scheduled to begin in fall of 2008. The mouth of the San Bernard could never be reached by vehicle—the ICW prevents that—although it was once possible to drive the beach from Sargent. Now that the river is closed, the water coming downstream and hitting the ICW will start cutting outlets through the beach below the Cedar Lakes.

The portion of the San Bernard between the end of its channel and the ICW can be reached by boat, and it is a popular spot for boaters to overnight. The beach at the mouth is pleasant, when the mosquitoes aren't too bad, and fishing can be good. There are boat ramps on the river upstream, but no bait camps as of this writing. FM 2918 runs from FM 521 down the west side of the river all the way to the ICW.

A group of residents and others interested in the San Bernard are trying to get the funds and permits to have the mouth reopened. To learn more of their efforts, go to www.friendsofthesanbernard.com. When the river is allowed to flow into the Gulf, the San Bernard can be an excellent stream for speckled trout in winter, under dock lights or those powered by a generator. Bull reds are found at the mouth in late summer and fall, and flounder are possible nearly any month.

Caney Creek joins the ICW at Sargent, and a cut to the Gulf from the ICW gets most of its flow from the creek. This is a man-made cut that at one point almost eroded the whole beach south of the ICW, but it has all been rebuilt. Caney Creek is noted for redfish, but it also offers good speckled trout fishing, especially at night under lights. Trout are taken under lights in winter when tides are not excessively low or freshwater run-off not excessively high. "Rat" reds roam the creek in the fall, and flounder are best in spring and fall migrations. To reach Caney Creek, take FM 457 south off FM 521 to Sargent.

20 Colorado River Area

At one time there was a cut to the Gulf from East Matagorda Bay known as **Brown Cedar Cut,** just south of Sargent. Accessible only by a long drive down Matagorda Peninsula, Brown Cedar was famous as a wade-fishing area on both the bay and the surf side. At various times the cut was closed by storm tides, then opened again by others. Brown Cedar has been closed for a long time, and it appears it will remain that way—short of a major storm making a direct hit—as efforts to get permission to dig it out over the years have failed. I mention Brown Cedar because even though it is closed, fishing on the bay side is still very good, due to the several coves and guts formed by currents through the years. Because it still takes either a long drive down the beach or a boat ride to reach, Brown Cedar qualifies as a legitimate hard-to-reach and special fishing hole. Warm weather is best for wade fishing the bay behind brown cedar, and fall is prime for the Gulf surf in front. Although this spot is always fairly secluded, those wishing a quiet spot to contemplate navels or otherwise get away from it all while doing some fishing will find it very private in winter months.

The bayfront at Palacios, showing some of the bayfront walkway and public piers.

Colorado River Area, Port O'Connor Area

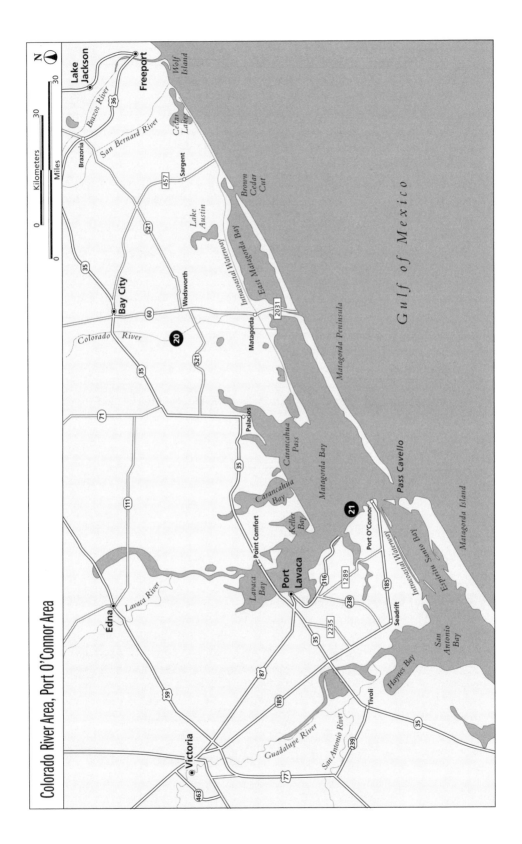

The **Colorado River** splits East and West Matagorda Bays and the Matagorda Peninsula. The Colorado is a famous winter speckled trout spot, and residents upriver make excellent catches off private docks under bright lights. The river also has a little-known striped bass fishery, with most catches coming from the saltwater barrier near Bay City. The mouth of the river is jettied, with a pier constructed to allow easy access to the jetties for anglers on foot, but the area was damaged by a tropical storm and may take some time to rebuild. Reds and other fish, such as Spanish mackerel, speckled trout, various panfish, and sharks, are common catches off the jetties.

The small town of Matagorda, at the junction of the Colorado River and the ICW, has various bait camps and boat ramps, as well as a new marina on the ICW. When I worked in this area, a friend who grew up there described Matagorda as "not the end of the world, but you can see it from there!" You have to want to go to Matagorda—there is nowhere else to reach just passing through—but there are reasons to want to go there. Several boat ramps and bait camps are located between Matagorda and the mouth of the river as well. Highway 60 leads south to Matagorda from Highway 35 at Bay City or from FM 521 at Wadsworth. While the channel between the jetties is subject to sanding, offshore access is possible here.

Farther down Matagorda Bay, west of the Colorado River, the Tres Palacios River runs into the bay of the same name near the town of Palacios. It is a shallow area, good for reds and flounder. When the bay is salty and clear, winter fishing for trout can be very good, because nearby Matagorda Bay is one of the deepest on the Texas coast.

The **Lavaca River** runs into Lavaca Bay across from the city of Port Lavaca. This is another shallow bay, and very underutilized by any anglers other than the locals. Shallow bays such as Lavaca can be almost dry under a north wind and a low winter tide, so they are best fished when spring renews them with a supply of salty water from the Gulf. Redfish and flounder are the main targets of such shallow water, but speckled trout will be found when the clarity indicates a good salinity level. It is just off Highway 35.

21 Port O'Connor Area

Port O'Connor is another of those places on the Texas coast where it is said you have to want to go there—you won't reach it just passing through. Port O'Connor is reached from Highway 35 via County Road 185, and it is the gateway to two fine passes. The Port O'Connor jetties frame the outlet of the Matagorda Ship Channel, a man-made cut through the western end of Matagorda Peninsula. Accessible only by boat, these jetties are often credited with being the Gulf outlet for offshore fishing and shrimping excursions, as well as Gulf oil-industry expeditions, but fishing along the jetties is also notable. Trout, redfish, and even offshore species like king mackerel feed here. Anglers from the metropoltan and coastal areas to the northeast make pilgrimages to Port O'Connor from early spring through late fall.

Pass Cavallo is the natural pass between Matagorda Island and the Matagorda Peninsula. It is a shallow pass that can only be navigated by extremely shallow-draft boats, and wading is a bit dangerous due to currents. Fishing is excellent in the vicinity of the pass for everything from trout to tarpon. And it's best in spring and again in the fall. Summer on the Gulf can be a searing experience in an open boat, unless fishing early or late in the day. It goes without saying that Pass Cavallo can also only be reached by boat.

The **San Antonio River** and the **Guadalupe River** run into San Antonio Bay between the towns of Seadrift and Austwell. San Antonio is another shallow bay that does not get as much attention as other spots but has good potential. These rivers are most noteworthy to coastal anglers for providing freshwater to the bays, but locals fish them for freshwater catfish and big alligator gar in the summer months. Redfish will venture farther into brackish streams than speckled trout, as will croaker, and are possible targets through the winter.

22 Port Aransas Area

Past Pass Cavallo, where Matagorda Island has morphed into San Jose Island, there is a natural pass between that piece of land and Mustang Island. In a confusing bit of nomenclature, the actual town called Aransas Pass is located on the mainland, while the city on the west side of the pass, on the island, is named Port Aransas.

Like most jetties, this jettied pass offers deeper water for rock walkers and excellent fishing. Because of the southerly latitude and clear water, warm-water species like tarpon are more common and large sharks abound. Speckled trout and reds are a given, as they are around all jetties, and migratory pelagics like king mackerel not only come in close enough to be caught by rock walkers at times, but also show up sooner than at points to the north. Due to the warmer weather and corresponding water temperatures, this area can be good for most species—trout, reds, flounder, and panfish—all year, although the migratory offshore mackerel will head for deeper water in winter.

This is still a part of the Texas coast where Highway 35 leads to all things salty. The "jetty boat" ferries passengers to San Jose Island, where they can get to the jetty. On the "Port A" side, getting to the jetty is much easier—just follow the signs. Port Aransas has tackle and baits shops, restaurants, motels, and RV parks.

Corpus Christi Bay is fed by a combination of streams. The **Frio River** runs into Choke Canyon Reservoir, then joins with the **Nueces River** to feed Lake Corpus Christi before the combined steam flows into Corpus Christi Bay. Corpus Christi Bay is deep enough to hold trout and reds all winter, and this will also be the time of year with the least boat traffic.

23 Bottom of the Coast

The hypersaline condition of the Lower Laguna Madre is due to the fact that there are no major rivers emptying into this bay and only two passes. The **Arroyo Colorado**, however, does end in the Laguna between Port Mansfield and Port Isabel, with fishing camps and a marina on its banks. Located on County Road 2925, past

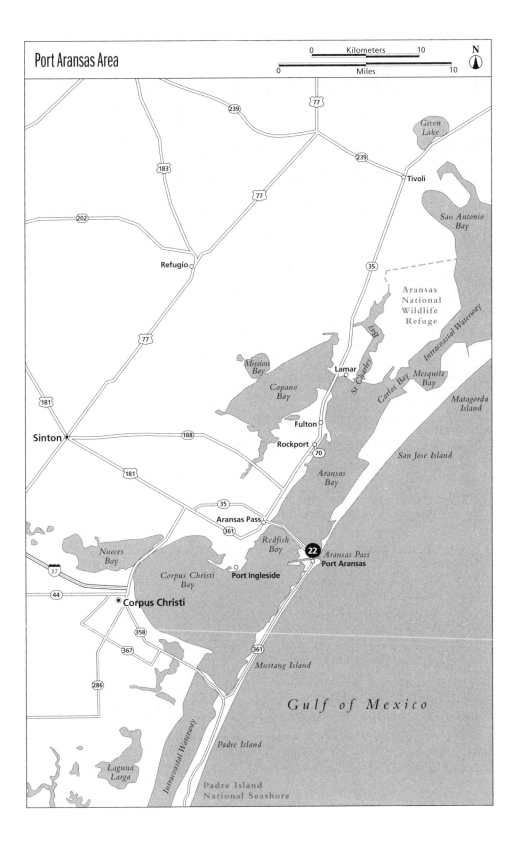

Arroyo City, this is one of the few public-access spots on the Lower Laguna. Wade fishing for trout here can be excellent in warm months, and reds will feed on the flats almost year-round. Anglers wanting a shot at a snook will be better served when water temperatures approach bath comfort—usually late spring through fall.

Port Mansfield is another public area in the midst of the giant King and Kennedy Ranches. It is the jumping-off point to the **Mansfield Cut,** a man-made channel through Padre Island. This is a jettied pass used for Gulf access, but the jetties are prime for tarpon, snook, specks, and reds. Because deep water is much closer here, offshore species are common catches in warm weather. The Mansfield Cut can be reached by boat from Port Mansfield or by four-wheel-drive vehicle coming down the beach from North or South Padre. Port Mansfield has marinas, bait camps, boat ramps, and lodging. Mansfield is good any time of year the wind will allow a boat to enter the bay, or cross it to the Gulf, except when extreme winter low tides drain the flats along the ICW.

On the southern tip of South Padre Island is **Brazos Santiago Pass,** the jettied outlet of the Brownsville Ship Channel. These jetties are called Brownsville or Port Isabel jetties. The east side of this pass can be reached from Port Isabel via the Queen Isabella Causeway—if it hasn't been shut down again by a barge colliding with the bridge. Port Isabel is a modern resort city with all the amenities this implies. South Padre Island is a beach resort popular with college students from all over the country on spring break, so those weeks in March are a good time to be somewhere else. Like Port Aransas, this is an area populated with serious anglers,

Fishing on the Brownsville Jetty, Boca Chica side. Offshore species and large jewfish have been caught here.

Bottom of the Coast

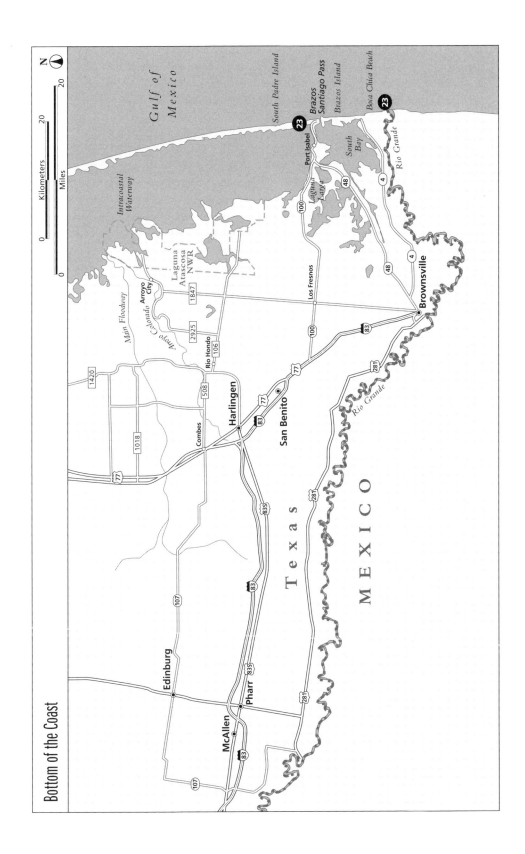

N

Kilometers
0   20
Miles
0   20

Gulf of Mexico

Intracoastal Waterway

South Padre Island

Port Isabel
23

Brazos Santiago Pass
Brazos Island

Boca Chica Beach
23

Laguna Madre

South Bay

Rio Grande

100

48

4

48

4

Laguna Atascosa NWR

1847

Arroyo City

Arroyo Colorado

Main Floodway

2925

Rio Hondo

106

Los Fresnos

100

Brownsville

83

281

Rio Grande

77

508

Harlingen

1420

1018

Combes

77

San Benito

77

835

835

281

MEXICO

Texas

107

Edinburg

Pharr

835

83

281

McAllen

83

107

and they have ample opportunity to enjoy their sport. A very temperate area, fishing is best when crowds are smallest, which would be winter and fall. Anything from speckled trout to snook and tarpon might be encountered in this area. The other side of Brazos Santiago Pass is reached by driving down Boca Chica Beach, as discussed in the Special Places chapter, and these jetties are great for fishing, as mentioned there.

A short drive down the beach to the west is the mouth of the **Rio Grande**, the legendary river marking the international border between Texas and Mexico. Had John Wayne known of the great fishing in this area, he might have taken some time off from all those cowboy movies set on the Rio to wet a line! This is big-fish territory, with trophy tarpon, monster sharks, line-stretching snook, and giant Goliath groupers in the jetty rocks. With the glitter of South Padre—the "Texas Riviera"—and the lure of Matamoras, Mexico, just across the border, this is an area worth devoting some time to.

The Bays

Although a drive down the Texas coast will reveal people fishing in every ditch, off every bridge, and in front of every culvert, the vast majority of Texas saltwater anglers pursue their sport in the bays. There are over twenty named main bays and many more smaller bays and tidal lakes along the Texas coastline, some behind barrier islands, some hiding behind a peninsula, some inshore and connected to the Gulf by a pass—but all are protected from the open Gulf, and all hold fish. Whether you drive to the edge of a bay and wade right in, or fish off a pier, or use a boat to reach more remote water, Texas bays will give you angling experiences to rival those found anywhere. With the length of the state's coastline and the number of bays available, even an ardent angler could spend a lifetime and probably never cover all this water.

Oyster reefs, like these exposed by a very low tide, are fish-attracting magnets in Texas bays.

24 Sabine Lake

Sabine Lake is a relatively shallow bay fed by the Neches River on the Texas side and the Sabine River on the Louisiana side. The Intracoastal Waterway (ICW) crosses the northern edge as the Sabine-Neches Canal. The lake runs only 2 to 5 feet deep along the edges, 6 to 8 feet in the center. The outlet to the Gulf is through Sabine Pass, a natural pass that has been jettied and is used for commercial shipping as well as for recreational and commercial fishing purposes.

The city of Port Arthur is on the southeast shore of the lake, Bridge City is on the north, and Orange is just a short distance up the Texas side of the Sabine River. Highway 87 runs to the lake from Bridge City or Orange to the north and from High Island to the south—if it were open from High Island. The oldest and best-known bait camp and launch is Bob Bailey's Camp in Bridge City, on Old River Cove, near where Old River Bayou enters. It is reached from Bridge City by taking Lake Street off Highway 87. Bailey's has a store, live and dead bait, and guide services. There was once also an infamous honky-tonk on the property.

Pleasure Island, on the west bank, was created by digging the Port Arthur Ship Channel to Sabine Pass. It features a large park area, at least four fishing piers, and a marina with a boat ramp that leads to the lake. There is a bridge to the island at the end of Highway 73 in West Port Arthur, and another crossing to Louisiana at the end of the lake, where the road number changes to 82 as it continues into the Pelican State. SGS Causeway Bait & Tackle is located near the bridge, and Parrothead Marina on the island has both gasoline and diesel. JEP's Emporium, on the Port Arthur side of the canal, sells gasoline along with dead bait and supplies.

Sabine Lake has a lot of oyster shell bottom, and it is garnering a reputation for large speckled trout, which are caught fishing under birds working over bait on the lower end of the lake. It has always been a hot spot for flounder, as evidenced by the current state record having been caught here. Redfish are also found in good numbers, and a glance at the state records list reveals that several species of what are normally considered freshwater catfish have been caught here, most likely in the upper coves after both rivers were running high. Boaters who want to fish the Louisiana side should check current regulations to be sure a Louisiana license is not required, as this situation changes from time to time. Sabine can be good in winter if the water isn't too fresh, or too low from winter tides. The lake is sensitive to both extremes, probably more so than to temperatures, although the shallow water is not attractive to trout when temperatures drop to near freezing. This means spring and fall are the most consistent fishing seasons here.

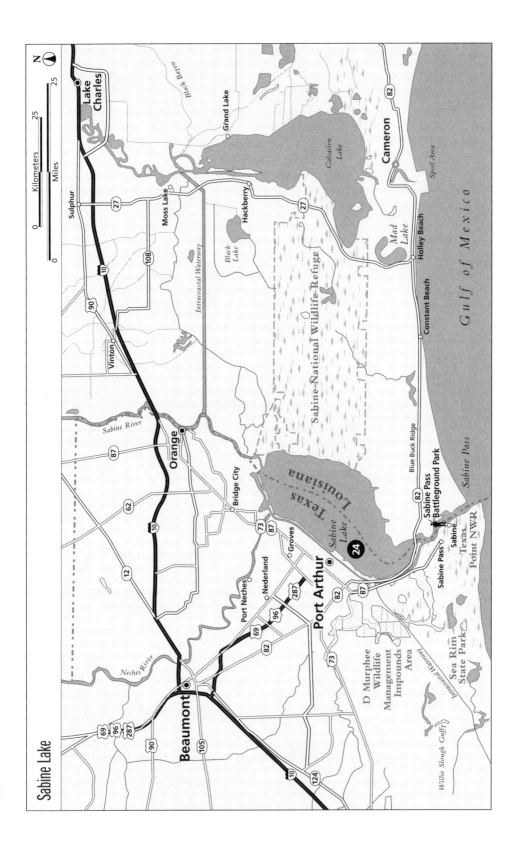

Sabine Lake

Galveston Bay System

The largest bay system in Texas is composed of East Bay, Trinity Bay, Galveston Bay, West Bay, and Chocolate Bay. The system can also include Christmas Bay (site 30) and Bastrop Bay (site 31) as they are connected to West Bay. Very close to metropolitan Houston, these bays are popular with both local and visiting anglers but still have room for newcomers. They also offer some of the most consistent bay fishing in the state, possibly aided by having three significant passes to the Gulf that allow water exchange and fish migration between them.

25 East Bay

East Bay is reached from Port Arthur by taking Highway 73 to Winnie, then going down Highway 124 to join Highway 87 west. From Beaumont to the north or the Houston area to the south, exit Interstate 10 at Winnie to Highway 124. From Galveston Island, take the Bolivar ferry across to the Bolivar Peninsula, again on Highway 87. Rollover Pass connects East Bay to the Gulf and has boat ramps and bait camps, plus an RV park. The portion of East Bay directly behind the pass is often referred to as Rollover Bay, although it is more of a large cove crossed by the ICW.

East Bay behind Rollover is shallow, with only 1 to 3 feet of depth showing on the charts. It is still an excellent wade-fishing area along the shorelines, especially when they are protected from the winds that roil the open bay. Wade fishing immediately behind Rollover is also good, although currents very near the pass can be strong during moving tides. There is also a boat ramp at the point where the ICW and Rollover Bay intersect. Both the north and south shorelines are fed by several bayous, which are always good spots to intercept flounder and redfish, but a shallow-draft boat is needed to reach these spots. A small boat cut to the ICW allows access to Stingaree Marina and Way Out Marina, where bait and ramps are found, plus there's also a pretty good restaurant at Stingaree.

East Bay deepens somewhat as it nears Galveston Bay, going to 4 to 6 feet in depth, and this part has many oyster reefs that attract fish and also some standing oil platforms with shell pads that function as artificial reefs. The north shoreline all the way to Smith Point is well-known for good fishing. Hanna's Reef, in the middle of the bay, is one of the traditionally better spots. The entire south shoreline is recognized for wade fishing, but again requires a boat for access because it is cut off from the main peninsula by the ICW. Back in the ICW from Bolivar Roads, Shirley's Bait Camp is the first and best-known facility. A run farther up the "ditch" takes you to the Bolivar Bait Camp across from Siever's Cove, where shallow-draft boats can enter the bay again. All of these bays will be similar as to species and seasons, except where noted that a particular bay—like Trinity—is more affected by freshwater runoff. Most targeted species will be redfish, flounder, and speckled trout.

East Bay, Trinity Bay, Galveston Bay, West Bay, Chocolate Bay

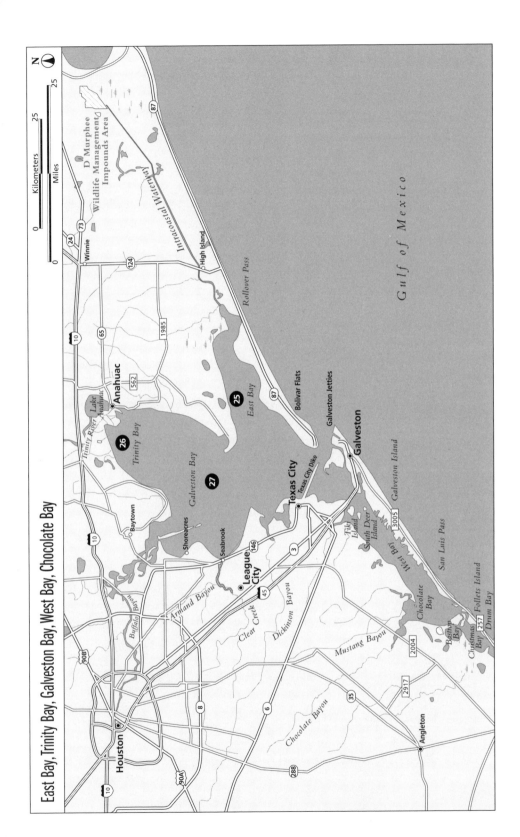

Best times will normally be spring through fall, although there can be good winter fishing when tides and water conditions are "right."

26 Trinity Bay

Trinity Bay lies north of East Bay and is reached by road from the city of Anahuac or by taking Highway 562 south from Anahuac to Smith Point. It is possible to launch at the Trinity River Bridge under Interstate 10 and follow the river to the bay, or launch at Fort Anahuac Park or Beason Park in Anahuac. Robbin's Park at Smith Point has a ramp, but it involves a lot of driving to reach. Childress Park, located at the end of Frankland Road off Highway 562 before reaching Robbins, has bait but no ramp.

There are also bait camps and boat ramps outside of Baytown. From Baytown, take Highway 146 to Spur 55 and head east to Tri-Cities Beach Road 2354. This road runs down the shoreline to Cedar Point, then curves with the bay to nearly Point Barrow. Thompson's Fishing Camp is on the point between Tabb's Bay and Ash Lake on Sims Road. This is near where the Cedar Bayou Channel exits land (Cedar Bayou) and cuts across above Atkinson Island to the east side of Galveston Bay. Across Ash Lake via a small bridge is Crawley's Bait Camp, an area institution.

While the northwest shoreline does have reefs and flats that are very fishable, this is a residential area with little public access, except by water. Launch facilities are also found on Cedar Bayou at the Baytown Marina on Kilgore Road, Roseland Public Boat Ramp on Highway 146, and the new Bayland Marina on Highway 146 just off the new Fred Hartman Bridge from La Porte. Many anglers who fish the bay regularly launch on the Galveston Bay side and make the run across to Trinity by boat. The middle of Trinity Bay is much deeper than East Bay, running 7 to 8 feet, and can be excellent in the fall for chasing trout working under birds.

The east shoreline of Trinity is prime wade-fishing territory for speckled trout. It has several prominent oyster reefs and some pronounced flats; it's fed by several tidal bayous. Perhaps more importantly, residential development is minimal and commercial development almost nonexistent. The northern end of the bay, where the Trinity River enters, is also a shallow area perfect for wading. Not far to the west is an area known as Jack's Pocket, and just past there is the discharge for the Houston Lighting and Power plant cooling pond. The warm water exiting this pond holds all sorts of fish in cool weather. The majority of the western shoreline is taken up by residential housing and a public park with no ramp or bait camp.

Several guide services specialize in fishing Trinity, and as with any Texas bay, hiring a guide to show you around before fishing it on your own can be a wise investment. The HL&P Spillway area is good in winter for what are normally warm weather species—reds and trout, mostly. Trinity is a favorite spot for speckled trout anglers from spring through fall, except when floodwaters coming down the Trinity River render the water too fresh.

27 Galveston Bay

Galveston Bay proper is the largest bay in the system, the distance across it from Texas City to East Bay being 30 miles. The western shore is very industrial, with refineries and chemical plants in Texas City, Baytown, and Bayport, near La Porte. Also on the western shore is Clear Lake, which has the largest concentration of recreational boats per acre outside of Fort Lauderdale, Florida. The bay has suffered from industrial and residential pollution but still offers good fishing, even up into Clear Lake and the several small brackish lakes that split off of it.

The northern end from Morgans Point through La Porte to Shoreacres is reached by road using Loop 410, off of Highway 146. The Morgans Point Flats are fishable by boat, and Sylvan Beach has a fishing pier and wading areas, in addition to bait and a boat ramp. There are good flats on both sides of the Houston Yacht Club entrance in Shoreacres and on either side of the new Bayport Ship Channel. Pine Gulley Park on Toddville Road, which is sort of a continuation of Loop 410 after the ship channel, has a fishing pier for public use. Just to the south are the Seabrook Flats, a good wading area where a couple of speckled trout several pounds larger than the state record were caught and weighed on certified scales but never submitted for consideration. Boat ramps are located under the Highway 146 bridge on the Clear Creek Channel.

The Kemah Flats and Bacliff Flats lead southward to the Houston Lighting and Power Company cooling canal outlet, a warm-water outflow good for winter

The Texas City Dike is a long jetty with a paved road and beaches on the north side.

fishing. There is an RV park and fishing pier here as well as a public park area. The San Leon Flats and San Leon Reef, just offshore, stretch to Eagle Point, home to the San Leon Marina and Eagle Point Fishing Camp. Jutting to the south is April Fool Point on the edge of Dickinson Bay, where the April Fool Point bait camp is located. Another boat ramp can be found on Dickinson Bayou above the bay, where Highway 146 crosses, along with Hillman's Marina and Restaurant.

Below Dickinson Bay is the entrance to Moses Lake and Dollar Bay, which is shallow but capable of holding fish. On the Texas City shore of Moses Lake you will find the Moses Lake Marina and Ray's Marina and Bait Camp. Just at the northern end of Bay Street, which runs along the bayfront in Texas City, is the Dollar Point Marina.

The main attraction in Texas City is the Texas City Dike, a huge jetty built during the WPA days to protect the Texas City Ship Channel. The dike can be driven to its end, some 11 miles, and fished nearly the entire length. Dike Road turns off Bay Street, and there are several bait camps just off the mainland. Running on the north are the Texas City Dike Flats, which can be waded and even have a public beach farther down the dike. A public boat ramp is located near the spot where a dry-stack marina once operated, and the Texas City Lighted Pier is at the end. The deep hole off the end of the pier produces big black drums during their spawning runs and sometimes offshore fish, like jack crevalles, that wander into the Houston Ship Channel from Galveston. The south side of the dike is rocky and the water is deep, as the ship channel runs close.

A lighted pier on the very end of the Texas City Dike allows a long cast to reach the deep water of the Houston Ship Channel.

Galveston Bay System

Just northwest of the intersection of the Trinity River Channel and the Houston Ship Channel is a spot known as Redfish Island. Redfish was once a popular picnic and overnight anchorage for sailors and powerboaters, and offered some wade-fishing opportunities, but it was washed away by Hurricane Alicia in 1983. It has been rebuilt by the U.S. Army Corps of Engineers and should be a good fishing destination—at least during midweek, when boat traffic is minimal—due to its proximity to the deep water of the two channels. The spoil bank formed by dredging the Houston Ship Channel and the channel itself is good, especially in cold or hot weather, when it provides a more stable temperature for trout, but boaters need to watch for large ships approaching. These oceangoing vessels will "suck" all the water off the shallow area, and when it comes back, it can cause a huge wave that might swamp a fishing boat.

Below Texas City, still on the west side of Galveston Bay, is Swan Lake, then the wadeable Virginia Flats, which run to the Galveston Causeway. On the south side of Galveston Bay, Offatts Bayou cuts into Galveston Island from the ICW just west of the causeway from the mainland. Offatt's is accessed by road from the island, and has a boat ramp on 61st Street at a public park with bait camps next door. Offatt's is known for the Moody Gardens amusement complex located at its western end and for excellent winter fishing for trout and redfish. Offatt's was greatly enlarged by dredging to raise Galveston Island after the terrible hurricane of 1900, which killed thousands of people. It runs to 30 feet deep in some spots, providing an excellent place for trout to gather during cold weather.

There is deep water near the Galveston Yacht Basin and Bolivar Roads, and some local enthusiasts fish for huge stingrays in this area. A large wreck known locally as the "concrete ship" provides fish-holding structure near the ship channel. Pelican Island—home to Sea Wolf Park, which has a vintage submarine on display—has a riprap bank and a public fishing pier. It is reached from Galveston Island off Harborside Drive, but boaters can work the shoreline by water for both drum and flounder during their respective spawning runs. The closest ramps are at the yacht basin.

28 West Bay

Like most Texas bays, West Bay runs deeper in the middle, but only 5 to 6 feet. The shorelines are shallower and are excellent wading areas. The north shore is undeveloped and accessible only by boat for the most part, except for a new canal subdivision called Harborwalk and the Teakwood marina and bait camp near the causeway bridge on Tiki Island. Tiki is actually a small peninsula that has so many canals cut in it, it is more water than land. The water behind Tiki is known as Jones Bay.

The south shoreline of Galveston Island has several canal subdivisions with marinas, bait camps, and boat ramps, such as Sea Isle, Terramar Beach, Jamaica Beach, and Bay Harbor. These split off from State Highway 3005, the San Luis Pass Road. There are several reefs in this bay, including a man-made "fish haven" constructed of old tires filled with concrete and placed over pilings that stand well above the bay's surface, making it easy to locate visually.

On the eastern end, just west of the causeway, North Deer Island and South Deer Island are perhaps best-known as bird rookeries but also offer fish-holding structure on the very edge of the deep water of the ICW. North Deer is approximately 144 acres, South Deer a little smaller, and both have significant shoreline area. The ICW runs against the north edge of North Deer, and a channel cuts between the two islands. There are many reefs in this area, the most well-known being Confederate Reef.

Although much of West Bay is too deep for wading, drifting and fishing under birds is excellent for trout. The shallow edges are good areas for flounder as well. The back side of Galveston Island State Park has a lot of good wading potential.

On the western end of West Bay, behind San Luis Pass, is the best fishing area in this bay. It is accessible only by boat, except for the bank immediately behind the San Luis Pass Toll Bridge to Follets Island, where bank-fishing and wade-fishing spots can be reached by car. There is a county park with a ramp and a lighted fishing pier on the Follets Island side of the pass. The channel from the Gulf under the San Luis Pass bridge can be as deep as 25 feet but shallows quickly, and the bar in the middle of the inside pass is very shallow.

Behind San Luis Pass, sandbars block access for deep-draft vessels but also attract and hold fish, providing excellent wade fishing, especially when the water is clear enough to easily distinguish the guts between the bars. There is sometimes a channel running through these bars, but the strong currents in the area change the formation of the bottom. The channel is occasionally marked by local boaters with lengths of PVC pipe, but these cannot always be trusted. The sandbars and the cuts between them are excellent structure for trout, redfish, and flounder, and sometimes open-Gulf species like jack crevalle come through.

A deep channel comes into the pass that bears to the west and runs between Mud Island and Bird Island. A deep-enough hole exists beside Bird Island to make it a prime spot for ambushing monster-size stingrays, and sometimes big sharks. Tarpon come through the pass as well. Another deep channel bears west before Cold Pass, which many old-timers say was originally named Coal Pass because barges used to offload coal cargoes here in the late 1800s, when the ill-fated city of San Luis was still in existence. This channel goes through Christmas Bay to a cut that was dug by an oil company and leads to the ICW. Most of the other channels "dead-end" before reaching the deeper water of the bay.

For many years I ran an offshore boat out of Chocolate Bayou and made occasional trips through San Luis Pass, but the bottom formation changed so fast, it was not a dependable Gulf outlet from West Bay. Past Mud Island is Mud Cut, a shallow passage through to Christmas Bay. The outlet on the West Bay side is very shallow, making it a good bet for flounder.

The ICW is the northern boundary between West Bay and Chocolate Bay. On the West Bay side, boaters can cross in and out of the canal at will, but the Chocolate Bay side is where the spoil from the canal dredging was deposited. This is now an area of oyster reefs, good for wading or fishing from a boat but very shallow and tough on boat bottoms and outboard lower units. Shrimp boats pull their nets in the deeper waters of the canal on hot summer days, bringing up sport fish as well as bait. The north shoreline before Chocolate Bay is cut by the ICW at Alligator Head. The bay side is a good fishing area under most conditions, and inside on the ICW is a very protected spot for windy days. West Bay holds all the normal Texas bay species—speckled and sand trout, redfish, flounder, gafftop catfish, and panfish species. It is best fished in spring through fall, as it is shallower than Galveston Bay proper, making it sensitive to low winter tides and hot summer temperatures.

29 Chocolate Bay

One way to reach West Bay is through Chocolate Bayou, below Alvin, and Chocolate Bay. Chocolate Bay begins just south of the FM 2004 bridge, where there is a very good county launching ramp. Two marinas with launch facilities are up the bayou, one with a ramp and the other with a lift that does not require getting the boat's trailer in the water. Both are on FM 203, in the small community of Amsterdam.

There are deep holes in Chocolate Bayou's old bends that offer secluded fishing spots, and even overnight anchorages. One cove in particular is almost a sure bet for redfish, but that one will remain my secret—you'll have to look for it. Flounder are also frequent catches. The chemical plants on the bayou maintain barge docks that are lighted and have deep water to attract and hold fish. I took speckled trout, sand trout, redfish, and black drum in large numbers at these spots during the twenty-five years I lived on Chocolate Bayou. A deep, dredged barge channel leads from the chemical plants up the bayou to the ICW, and the islands and reefs all along this route hold good numbers of trout and redfish. The shallow flats just past the bridge are also good spots for flounder gigging at night.

In the widest part of Chocolate Bay, before it merges with West Bay, fishing opportunities are very good. Trout gather at an oyster reef—Long Reef—that runs down the center of this section of the bay, and the water on either side is deep enough for most boats to negotiate. On the northwest side of this section is the outlet of New Bayou, which can be negotiated to a low-water bridge maintained by an oil company to reach portions of their property. Redfish sometimes congregate in this bayou, and the mouth is a good spot for flounder on outgoing tides.

On the southeastern edge of Chocolate Bay is an entrance to Hall's Lake, a shallow area fed by Hall's Bayou. Flounder and redfish await boats that can get in this shallow lake. The western shore of Chocolate Bay is difficult to reach by boat—there is a narrow cut through the spoil bank that is not marked—but anglers who know the bay can get through and work the productive area near the bank by wading.

From Chocolate Bay to West Bay, the channel that enters and crosses the ICW can be tricky. A shallow triangle-shaped area has built up in the middle, with channels on the sides turning east and west. Tugs pushing barges routinely move the marker buoys, so the area should be negotiated slowly and cautiously. Chocolate Bay can be a fine place to be in spring, but really comes into its own in the fall, when redfish are especially numerous. Speckled trout are also found over oyster reefs in fall.

30 Christmas Bay

Cold Pass (aka Coal Pass) connects the portion of West Bay immediately behind San Luis Pass to Christmas Bay, a small, 1- to 3-foot-deep bay that is being recognized as an excellent wade- and drift-fishing venue. It is possibly the best bay on the upper coast to fly fish, and the bottom is mostly hard sand—perfect for wading. Kayakers also love Christmas, as they can drive from either Surfside or the San Luis Pass Toll Bridge on Highway 257 and park close enough to the water to carry their craft to launch. Along with the county park, Bright Light Grocery on Highway 257 has bait and supplies. A bit farther to the west on Highway 257 is Seidler's Landing, with a public boat ramp on a canal leading to Christmas Bay, and Ernie's Too, a bait camp.

Tailing reds, schooling trout under birds, and hefty flounder for either hook and line or gigging can all be found at different times here. Fishing the birds is good in fall and spring, when they chase shrimp that are also followed by speckled trout. Reds are at their very best in fall, and flounder giggers like to work the summer flats. Although Christmas Bay comes very close to the ICW, no navigable cut exists between the two. In addition to Cold Pass, Titlum Tatlum Bayou runs between Christmas Bay and West Bay, creating an isolated spit of land known as Moody's Island, and offers good fishing on either end during tidal flow.

Because of its shallow depth, Christmas may be almost dry during extreme low tides in winter, and boats in the bay when a strong north wind coincides with a falling tide should begin working their way out. This is true for any of the very shallow bays and saltwater lakes along the Texas coast.

31 Bastrop Bay

The northern end of Christmas Bay joins Bastrop Bay, another shallow body of water that is more isolated. There are no roads leading to Bastrop, and therefore no baits camps or launch ramps. Bastrop Bay can be entered either by crossing Christmas Bay on the narrow east end through a once-dredged channel known as "Oil Field Cut" past Christmas Point, or from the north, by the same channel from the ICW. Bastrop Bayou crosses the ICW, but boaters taking that route to Bastrop Bay may find the cut too shallow, in which case they should run the short distance west to the Oil Field Cut.

Bastrop Bay is dotted with oyster reefs and some spoil from the channel dredging, and it has a lot to offer shallow-water anglers looking to avoid crowds. Bastrop Bayou also has good fishing, along with a couple marinas offering launching and bait that are reached by turning off FM 2004 onto FM 227. The bayou channel runs fairly straight to the ICW, crossing several oxbows and a couple of shallow saltwater lakes—Cox Lake and Lost Lake—that can be worth a try. Bastrop Bayou and its bay are especially known for redfish. Fish for redfish and flounder in the fall, speckled trout in spring and summer.

Christmas Bay, Bastrop Bay

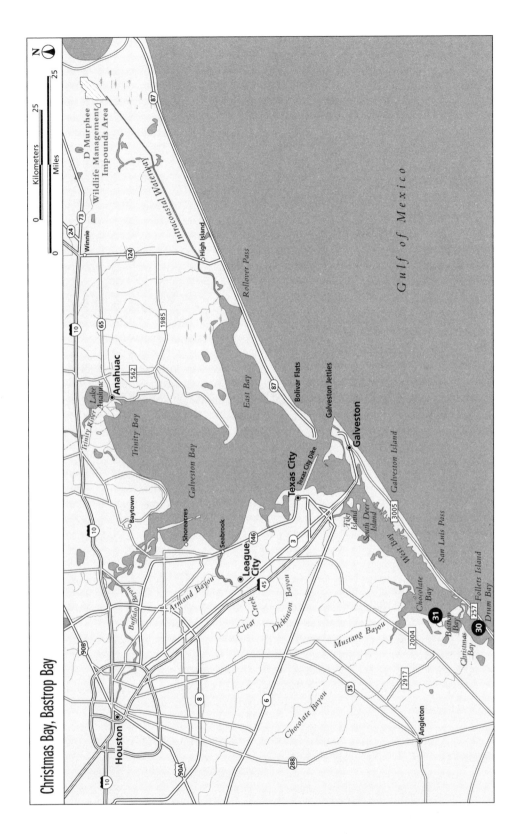

Freeport and Sargent Areas

Freeport proper is one of the few Texas coastal cities and shipping ports that is not located on a bay, but rather practically on the shore of the Gulf itself. Because of this, Freeport is thought of mainly as a destination for surf and offshore fishing. This makes it almost a secret inshore fishing mecca. Most of the best fishing will be in shallow lakes and marsh canals, in addition to tidal bayous and creeks, rather than open bays.

32 Drum Bay

This very shallow bay touches Christmas Bay on its eastern end and has a narrow opening into the ICW. Water depth is seldom over 2 feet, usually less, making this an area best suited for very shallow-draft boats or kayaks. Waders or kayakers can also reach the bay from Highway 257. When bank fishing these marshy areas, watch out for rattlesnakes on high ground, as well as small stingrays in the shallows.

A long finger of land runs roughly down the middle of Drum Bay, and an "entrance" to the lower bay is found at the western end, where the "Old Intracoastal" dead-ends. Lower Drum also has an entrance from the ICW, but this is very shallow water. Fishing the entrance to these shallow bays at the ICW on a falling tide is an excellent tactic, and avoids the risk of getting stuck in the mud. Because these bays are generally shallow and muddy, redfish and flounder are the dominant species, and fishing is best when spring or fall tides bring their water levels highest.

33 Nick's, Salt, and Swan Lakes

On the northern side of the ICW are several small, brackish lakes that could be worth exploring. Nick's Lake and Salt Lake are both connected by Salt Bayou and can only be reached by something like a kayak or canoe, but if the mosquitoes don't prove fatal, some great fishing can be found without much competition. There is also a good number of marsh ponds that mostly connect on high tides to the east of Nick's Lake. Fishing these lakes could be exciting and productive, but should be considered an "expedition" in terms of necessary preparation.

Swan Lake is south of the ICW and has an entrance from the canal. The entrance is a popular spot that can be reached by boat or you can brave driving: take CR 257, turn into the unnamed subdivision where the old Coast Guard station site sits just to the east, down the bank of the ICW. This spot also has a boat ramp in a protected harbor that is sanded in to a shallow depth but suitable for most bay boats. Again, shallow water favors reds and flounder, species that feed on the bottom and eat a lot of crabs and other small shellfish. High tides of spring and fall are the best times to access these waters.

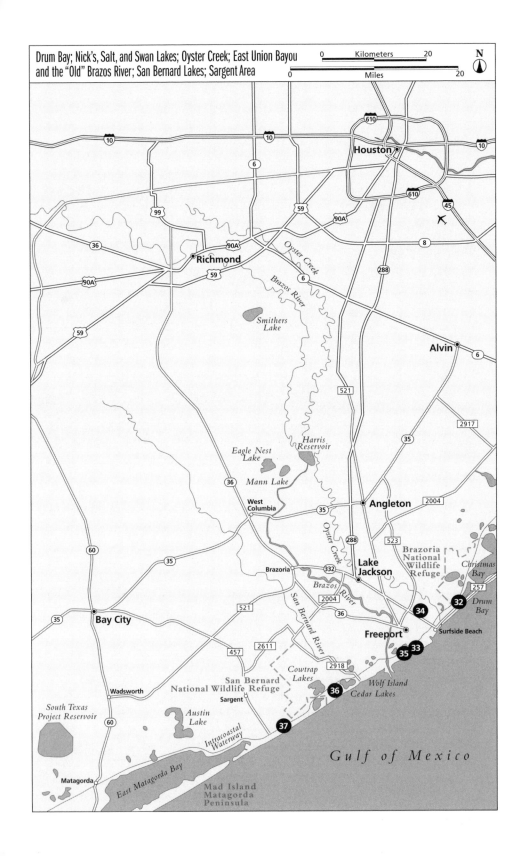

0   Kilometers   20
0   Miles   20

N

Houston

Richmond

Alvin

Smithers Lake

Oyster Creek

Brazos River

Harris Reservoir

Eagle Nest Lake

Mann Lake

West Columbia

Angleton

Oyster Creek

Brazoria National Wildlife Refuge

Christmas Bay

Lake Jackson

Brazoria

Brazos River

Drum Bay

34

32

Bay City

San Bernard River

Freeport

Surfside Beach

35

33

Cowtrap Lakes

Wolf Island Cedar Lakes

36

Wadsworth

San Bernard National Wildlife Refuge

Sargent

South Texas Project Reservoir

Austin Lake

Intracoastal Waterway

37

Gulf of Mexico

Matagorda

East Matagorda Bay

Mad Island Matagorda Peninsula

34 Oyster Creek

Oyster is a very long creek that originates near the city of Houston. It meanders quite a bit before joining the ICW, with several old oxbows that have been closed off from the main creek. There are three canal subdivisions, a marina, and a boat-yard on Oyster Creek that are reached from FM 523 by turning east on FM 792 before the small city of Oyster Creek. Large offshore fishing boats heading to the ICW depart frequently from these docks, so fishing on busy weekends can be hectic. On weekdays, however, the calmer creek holds fish in good numbers.

Boaters can enter from the ICW; a ramp on FM 523 is privately owned and not well maintained—don't use it. Kirby Marina and the canal subdivisions are private, but if permission is obtained to enter, fishing around the dock lights in winter can be excellent for speckled trout, though most fish will run on the small side. The city of Oyster Creek has a park just inside the city limits on FM 523 that features picnic areas, restrooms, and a lighted fishing pier.

There are two oxbows off the main creek that a bay boat can easily enter, though not many do. Bank fishing is also possible by taking shell roads off the pavement on the top of the storm levee that runs alongside Oyster Creek. At least one "fishing map" I consulted stated that the channel in Oyster Creek was "marked by privately maintained aids." These "aids" are milk jugs marking crab traps in the shallows and on the oyster reefs. They actually do function as channel markers, but do not get too close, as they will be on top of the reef rather than on the channel's edge. Speckled trout are numerous in winter, especially around lighted docks and piers. Redfish are best in the fall, over oyster reefs and in shoreline grass. Traffic from boats headed offshore early and coming in during late evening can make fishing difficult and unproductive on warm weather weekends.

35 East Union Bayou and the "Old" Brazos River

This small bayou sometimes shelters big fish, and the flooded marsh on the east side also has potential. The "Old" Brazos River was cut off many years ago from the main stream, and a new Gulf outlet for the river was dredged by the U.S. Army Corps of Engineers, leaving the old river as the Brazosport/Freeport shipping harbor. A city park at the very end has a small public boat ramp. Just before that, Mitchell's Bait Camp has a ramp, bait, fishing pier, and some dockage. There are fish in this part of the harbor, and I know anglers who have targeted mangrove snapper around docks and pilings here in winter. Parts of the harbor are off-limits to boaters, due to Homeland Security measures. A new ramp in Surfside allows boaters to launch in the Old Brazos channel between the Freeport jetties. The ramp is located near the Coast Guard station, off Ft.Velasco Boulevard.

Following the ICW west, there is a failed canal subdivision on the south bank just before the new bridge leading to Quintana and Bryan Beaches. This area offers some fishing opportunities, and it can be reached by car by taking County Road 1495 from Highway 288 and crossing the ICW on the new bridge. Past this bridge, a shallow cut leads to Bryan Lake on the north, another lake best fished in a kayak or possibly a flounder boat.

At the Brazos River, boaters can turn south to the mouth at the Gulf beach, or north to fish upstream. Bank anglers can start at the Highway 36 bridge just below the city limits of Freeport, then work their way down County Road 242A all the way to the gated property around the locks on the ICW, finding a boat ramp and several spots to park on the river bank to fish. Between the Highway 36 bridge and the FM 2004 bridge on the Brazos, most bay-type boats will have little trouble navigating upstream.

A park is located on the river bank in the city of Freeport, just past the high school's football stadium. There is an area very good for winter trout fishing upstream, but the river must be clear and the night cold. A boat with a generator to power lights, or a battery-powered "green light," will draw clouds of specks at times. A couple of warm-water outlets from Dow Chemical also hold fish in winter, including tarpon. Not much farther upstream is Sea Center Texas, a joint effort between Dow and Texas Parks & Wildlife, which has a fish hatchery and holding ponds, plus an aquarium and displays open to the public.

The river south of the ICW can hold jack crevalles and big sharks. It has also yielded a large number of tournament-winning gafftop catfish as well as trout, redfish, and flounder. As noted before, winter fishing is good for speckled trout, even tarpon at the warm-water discharge. Seasonally migratory fish such as jacks and sharks are always better in warmer months, even the heat of summer. Reds and flounder are plentiful in spring and fall.

36 San Bernard Lakes

Between the "New" Brazos and San Bernard Rivers, on the north bank, a series of small tidal lakes that are fed and joined by Jones Creek connect to the ICW. Jones Lake #1 opens on the ICW, and Jones Lakes #2 through #7 stretch upstream. These lakes are shallow and isolated—they cannot be reached by road. Just north of the ICW on the San Bernard River is the outlet of Redfish Bayou and McNeil Bayou, the latter of which widens to McNeil Lake and Pelican Lake.

Past the San Bernard River, between the ICW and the Gulf, are the Cedar Lakes—four of them connected in a line. These lakes are very shallow and might not be suitable for wading over most of their area due to soft bottom. Because they are connected to both the ICW and the Gulf—through a small channel cutting the beach from Fourth Cedar Lake—if they can be fished by shallow-draft boat, the results can be very worthwhile.

North of the ICW, Windmill Lake opens on the canal and has a shallow boat lane reported along the north bank. A bit farther to the west are the Cowtrap Lakes. East Cowtrap is small and probably of most value as a spot to ambush fish exiting to the ICW. Main Cowtrap has a boat lane leading from the ICW that heads well into North Cowtrap but does not go into West Cowtrap. There are numerous oyster reefs and some wading opportunities among the Cowtrap lakes.

Two areas on either side of the ICW consisting of interconnected marsh ponds are known as East and West Redfish Paradise, and they are aptly named. East Paradise drains into Cowtrap Lake, while West Paradise empties into Cedar Lake

Bayou, just before it joins the ICW across from the mouth of Fourth Cedar Lake. Around a bend in the ICW, continuing west, is the mouth of Salt Bayou.

Any of these tidal streams or lakes that empty into the ICW create opportunities to intercept fish coming out on a falling tide. None of these lakes can be reached by road. They are best reached by running a boat down the ICW from the Brazos River Highway 36 launch ramp or the ramp on the San Bernard at the ICW. These areas are good for flounder, panfish, and redfish any time the tide has pushed enough water in to hold fish or bait. Such areas are often most productive on a falling tide, when fish wait at the entrance to ambush bait coming out with the flow of water. If the bottom is hard enough for wading, a high tide will let reds roam into the grass after small crabs.

37 Sargent Area

Just before Sargent is the oxbow of Dead Caney Lake, which meets the ICW on both ends and also connects to man-made canals on the north. At one time it cut through the beach as a Gulf outlet. Caney Creek is famous for redfish in winter and speckled trout under lights in warmer months. There are several public ramps and a few bait camp/marinas in Sargent and on Caney Creek, which is reached by taking FM 457 south from FM 521.

Past Caney Creek, on the north bank of the ICW, are Journey Bayou and Boggy Bayou. Farther along is Chinquapin Bayou, which drains Lake Austin. There is a launch ramp on the bayou, on the end of Chinquapin Road, off of FM 521. Lake Austin is noted for shallow water and good fishing for reds. Like other shallow tidal lakes, water depth is the key to fishing, so high tides are preferable. Spring tides are among the best, fall a close second, and winter the worst. Various other tidal lakes are also found between Chinquapin and the Colorado River.

Matagorda to Corpus Christi

38 East Matagorda Bay

East Matagorda Bay can be accessed from Sargent through the new Caney Creek Cut or from the ICW through several rather shallow cuts: Third Cut, Fourth Cut, Turkey Slough Cut, Boggy Bayou Cut, and Old Gulf Cut. Those with four-wheel drive and a taste for adventure can drive the beach down Matagorda Peninsula from the mouth of the Colorado River to the Brown Cedar Cut area.

The cut to the Gulf has been closed for many years, but it is just a short walk across the dunes to the bay and excellent wade fishing. There are bait camps and launch ramps along the Colorado, from the town of Matagorda to the river's mouth. The county navigation district operates the Matagorda Marina, which has a ramp, bait, fuel, a restaurant, and wet boat slips. Boaters heading to the river from the marina must go through a swing bridge across the ICW, but those going to a cut to enter East Matagorda Bay have no such worry. This bridge is scheduled to be replaced with a fixed span bridge, although the date of construction has not been announced.

There are many oyster reefs in East Matagorda's shallow confines. The bay has nice wading areas along its shoreline and good drift fishing in the middle, plus action under feeding birds. At the western end, several bayous that are accessible by kayak dot the marsh between the river and the bay. East Matagorda Bay may be reached by boat from Sargent or by launching at the Matagorda Marina off Highway 60 or one of the ramps along the Colorado River on FM2031 and going into the bay through one of the cuts from the ICW, such as Old Gulf Cut or Boggy Bayou. Wade fishers can access the bay from the beach on Matagorda Peninsula, east of the Colorado River mouth. Speckled trout under birds or over reefs are good in spring and fall, even summer when temperatures are not too extreme. This is a shallow bay, so low winter tides limit access.

39 Western End of Matagorda Bay

Matagorda Bay—the part that locals call "West Matagorda Bay"—is easier to reach than its brother to the east, as the new Colorado River channel runs to it from the ICW. It can also be accessed from the Mad Island Reef channel, and the ICW enters the bay at the end of West Matagorda Bay.

Matagorda is also much deeper than East Matagorda, running to 12 feet in the main bay. The northern shore area is fairly free of bayous and sloughs, though it does have mud flats and oyster reefs. The southern shoreline of Matagorda Peninsula, however, is a constant interruption of cuts and bayous and coves, all providing good fishing opportunities. The peninsula is actually an island here, as the Colorado

East Matagorda Bay; Western End of Matagorda Bay; Matagorda Bay;
Lavaca Bay; Port O'Connor; Espiritu Santo Bay; San Antonio Bay

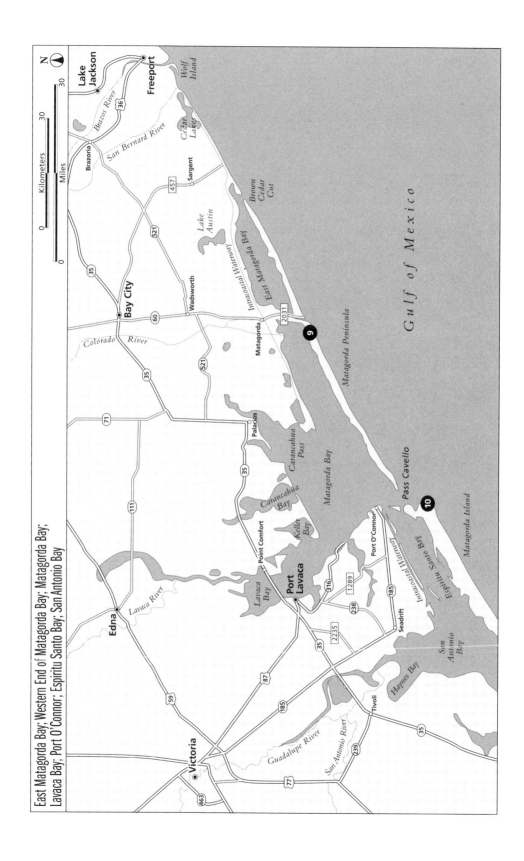

River cuts through it, consisting of private property used to graze cattle in winter, before the mosquitoes and rattlesnakes are out in force.

There are no ramps or bait camps on this portion of the bay. Many good oyster reefs and mud banks exist in West Matagorda, making it a favorite fishing area for experienced local anglers. It is also the bay where the most and largest tripletails in the state are caught. Key species are speckled trout, redfish, and flounder, with the exotic tripletail thrown in. Because this is a deeper bay, winter fishing for trout can be good over reefs. When tides are high, the shallow shoreline flats are good for trout and flounder, as well as reds in the grass. Fall is probably the best season, but no season is really bad here, given decent weather conditions.

40 Matagorda Bay

Matagorda Bay proper is a large body of water and deep by Texas bay standards. With the exception of Halfmoon Reef, which juts into the bay from Palacios Point, there are virtually no reefs in this bay except along the shorelines, and Halfmoon is 4 to 6 feet deep so it really can't be waded. This may be one reason the open bay is not as popular as many other Texas bays, especially with the many back bays in the general area. The 9- to 13-foot depths are dotted with active and submerged gas wells, however, which can offer very good structure fishing.

Spoil banks dot the western edge of the Palacios Ship Channel, which crosses Matagorda Bay from the north and joins the ICW about two-thirds of the way across the bay. There are also spoil banks on the bay side of the Matagorda Ship

The walkway south of the Palacios Community Pier passes clear bay water and more free rock-groin piers.

Channel, which runs back to the channels leading to the Port Lavaca and Point Comfort industrial zones. The Matagorda Peninsula bank has 10 to 14 feet of water butting against much shallower banks, mud flats, and sandbars, which is an excellent fishing situation.

At the northeastern corner of Matagorda Bay, Oyster Lake can be entered from the bay by Palacios Bayou or from the ICW as it prepares to exit Palacios Point. Tres Palacios Bay, fed by the small river of the same name, has shoreline reefs and a large spoil area on the west side of the Palacios Ship Channel. Turtle Bay, on the western side of Tres Palacios, is shallower, but it's still 3 to 4 feet deep. On the north shore of Matagorda Bay, Carancahua Bay is reached through a narrow pass. It has a couple small lakes leading up a long and fairly narrow main bay that has 4-foot depths all the way to Highway 35, where there are launch facilities but no bait camps. This part of the bay is reached best from the city of Palacios, on Highway 35, where there are several launch ramps and bait camps. Reds should be good in fall, as are flounder in the shallows. Good numbers of speckled trout stay in the deeper waters all year. Tripletail are a summer visitor.

41 Lavaca Bay

Lavaca Bay is named for the city of Port Lavaca, or maybe it was the other way around? It can be reached via the ship channel from Matagorda Bay, plus it is crossed by Highway 35 going into Port Lavaca. This bay has 4- to 9-foot depths, but it also has many reefs and flats. The Lavaca River Channel, the Port Lavaca Channel, and another channel leading to Point Comfort allow easy traveling by boat. There is also a channel leading into Chocolate Bay on the west side of the main bay.

Boat ramps are located in Port Lavaca and Point Comfort, at the Harbor of Refuge just above Chocolate Bay, and on Chocolate Bayou above the bay, on Buren Road off FM 238 (note that these are not the same Chocolate Bay and Bayou as those off West Galveston Bay). Port Lavaca is a good-size city that offers restaurants, motels, movie theaters, and shopping, as well as RV parks and a beach. The old Highway 35 bridge on either side of Lavaca Bay has been turned into fishing piers. Although hurricanes have battered their length down, they offer both non-boaters and boaters who wish to fish on bad-weather days an opportunity to reach reefs too far to wade to from shore. The piers are lighted at night, and there is a bait stand on the Port Lavaca side.

To the south, Powderhorn Lake is considered a top fishing spot. It can be reached by boat from Port O'Connor via Matagorda Bay, or by road by taking FM 238 to FM 316 south to "New" Indianola. The original settlement of Indianola was a thriving shipping port but was destroyed by hurricanes in the 1800s. There is a marina here, and Powderhorn RV Park is close by. Powderhorn Lake can also be reached where FM 1289 crosses on the way to Port O'Connor, though the ramp here is gravel and mainly just suitable for small boats. Anglers line the pier all through the winter, but spring and fall provide the cleaner water preferred by speckled trout. Reds and flounder inhabit the back areas of the bays and any tidal stream that enters them; their abundance is more dependent on tide and weather conditions than season of the year.

42 Port O'Connor

Port O'Connor (POC) is one of the most popular fishing areas for bay anglers on the Texas coast. Located at the convergence of Matagorda Bay, the ICW, and Espiritu Santo Bay (just across the ICW), POC is the gateway to an entire world of back-bay fishing in clear and wadeable water. Immediately outside the "little jetties" that protect the ICW's entrance, anglers based in POC can find good fishing conditions on the short trip to Matagorda Peninsula, where the Matagorda Ship Channel cuts through to the Gulf and the "big jetties" that protect that entrance.

There is good wade fishing on the back side of the peninsula, and the shoal water behind Pass Cavallo offers great drift fishing. Pass Cavallo is the gap between Decros Point on the end of the peninsula and Matagorda Island. This pass is very shallow but drops off fast on the Gulf side, where the fishing is good for trout, reds, and often tarpon. To fish the Gulf side, however, you must approach from the Gulf. The bay side of the pass has even deeper water and is easier to approach—by boat. The part of the peninsula between the jetties and Decros Point is an island, cut off from any other land, but can be a good place to camp and fish. Port O'Connor can be reached from Port Lavaca via County Road 1289 to FM 185, or by continuing past Port Lavaca on Highway 35 and taking FM 185 through Seadrift. Spring opens up the fishing, which holds well through summer, but really peaks with the fall.

43 Espiritu Santo Bay

Espiritu Santo Bay is best entered with a shallow-draft boat, which most area anglers are equipped with. Cuts exist from Matagorda Bay at Big Bayou (Mitchell's Cut) and Saluria Bayou, and from the ICW at Fisherman's Cut (across from Port O'Connor), the cut between Blackberry and Dewberry Islands, and another cut at Coyote Pass.

This bay is dotted with reefs and several islands, and there are also many gas platforms and wells. The eastern end is all coves, marsh, and bayous, and the north and south shores have islands cutting off lakes and small bays. Bayucos Island, Grass Island, and Farwell Island provide fishable shorelines. On the south, Pringle Lake, Contee Lake, Long Lake, and South Pass Lake are behind Vanderveer Island. Just outside Pringle Lake is a spot called the Army Hole, a deep hole created when the island was used as a bombing range by the military. It is now a famous cold-water fishing spot.

On the north side of the bay, Dewberry Island, Long Island, and Little Grass Island are in front of Shoalwater Bay and The Lagoon. As Espiritu Santo Bay merges with San Antonio Bay, more fishing territory is added by Steamboat Island, South Pass Island, and the Chain of Islands and their attendant reefs. An angler could spend a lot of time covering all this water properly. The most practical way to reach this bay is by launching a boat at Port O'Connor and coming down the ICW. The many small islands, coves, and bayous make it a redfish heaven, and flounder anglers should find it to their liking as well. Spring and fall, with their normally higher tides, are best for this area.

44 San Antonio Bay

San Antonio Bay is just past Espiritu Santo. Seadrift is the access point on the east side, Austwell on the west. Both are not far from Highway 35, which runs almost to the bay. It is fed by the San Antonio River and forms the shoreline of the Aransas National Wildlife Refuge, where endangered whooping cranes winter. The south shoreline is on Matagorda Island, with no vehicle access. Mesquite Bay, which has a very fishable north shoreline cut by the ICW, separates San Antonio Bay from Aransas Bay. Both trout and redfish can be found in what is a relatively lightly fished bay. Because it is a back bay and not exceptionally deep, access is best on higher spring and fall tides.

45 Aransas Bay and Copano Bay

The next large bay on the Texas coast is Aransas Bay, which is behind San Jose Island and joins San Antonio Bay on the east and Corpus Christi Bay on the west. On the east shore is Goose Island State Park, where there is boat ramp. Sea Gun, a weathered resort development with a small marina and ramp, is immediately off Highway 35 in the community of Lamar.

The Highway 35 bridge at Lamar crosses Copano Bay, which runs many miles inland and spins off into the smaller bays of Port Bay, which runs back behind Rockport—Fulton on the west, Mission Bay on the northeast. St. Charles Bay cuts to the east from the opening of Copano. There is a string of reefs running roughly from the bridge area to a spot on San Jose Island known as Paul's Mott. The entire island shoreline is a maze of shallow lakes, bayous, and marshes that can only be fished in a shallow-draft boat. Kayaks are becoming very popular to fish these kinds of locations, but in areas this far from roads, a transport vessel is required to get the little boats to the water.

Mud Island to the south combines with Traylor and Talley Islands and the marshy area of the Lighthouse Lakes to cut Aransas Bay off from Redfish Bay. The ICW cuts down the middle, then angles back to shore toward Corpus Christi, with an "alternate" channel running to the Gulf outlet at Port Aransas, just at Lydia Ann Island.

Highway 35 leads to the communities of Rockport and Fulton, a resort area known as a fishing and hunting jumping-off spot as well as an artists' retreat. Fulton has a fishing pier, a protected public ramp, and several RV parks and bait camps. In Harbor Oaks, on the edge of Rockport, Seabreeze Drive circles Little Bay and follows Ninemile Point. The canal subdivision of Key Allegro has a marina and is near several bait camps.

Rockport Harbor is a bit farther down on State Highway 70 and has a public boat ramp. The average 12-foot depth across Aransas Bay means boaters from Rockport can either follow the ICW to Port Aransas or cut straight across the bay. Cove Harbor Marina is just off the ICW, where it passes through the headland above Talley Island, and it too has a boat ramp. All the islands on the west end are good fishing grounds. This deeper bay is not as popular with Texas anglers, who

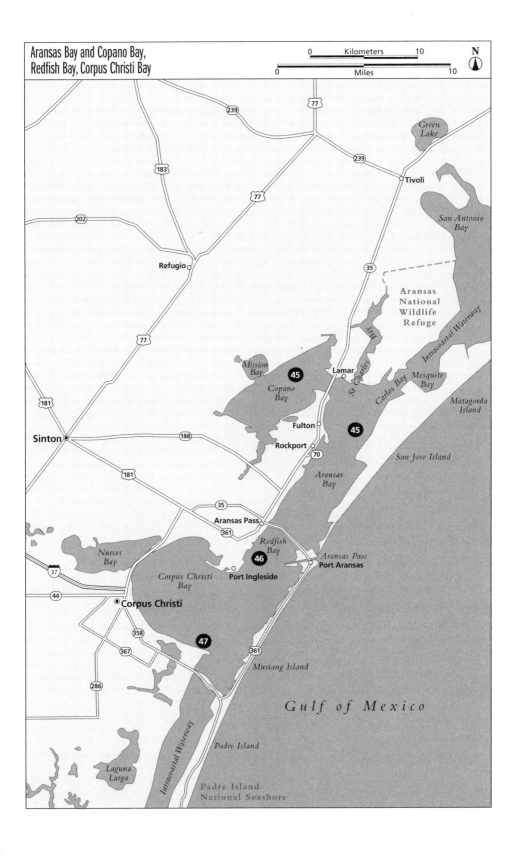

Kilometers

0   10

0   Miles   10

N

239

77

Green
Lake

239

183

Tivoli

77

San Antonio
Bay

202

35

Refugio

Aransas
National
Wildlife
Refuge

Intracoastal Waterway

77

Mission
Bay

45

Lamar

St. Charles Bay

Carlos Bay

Mesquite
Bay

Copano
Bay

Matagorda
Island

181

Sinton

188

Fulton

45

Rockport

70

San Jose Island

181

Aransas
Bay

35

Aransas Pass

361

Nueces
Bay

Redfish
Bay

46

Aransas Pass

Port Aransas

37

Corpus Christi
Bay

Port Ingleside

44

Corpus Christi

358

367

47

361

Mustang Island

286

Gulf of Mexico

Intracoastal Waterway

Padre Island

Laguna
Larga

Padre Island
National Seashore

like to wade and work reefs, but it has much to offer a boat fisher who looks for birds over bait in spring and fall or who just prospects for speckled trout and reds in other times of the year. The deeper water means good winter potential.

46 Redfish Bay

Palm Harbor Marina is the first boat ramp on Redfish Bay and the ICW past Talley Island. Redfish is much shallower—2 to 3 feet in most places—and has a lot of bay-grass beds. Several of these areas are now protected from damage by boat props, so there are marked boat lanes that vessels traveling through must follow. The Light-house Lakes area in South Bay is full of markers like these, leading through the maze of lakes, sloughs, bayous, and marshes. This area can be reached by kayakers launching along the partly man-made "peninsula" that leads across the bay from Aransas Pass to Harbor Island, across from Port Aransas, as long as they are very careful crossing the Aransas Channel with its heavy boat traffic.

This same spit of land effectively isolates Redfish Bay from Aransas Bay. The spots to cut through are the ICW crossings, where the submerged Corpus Christi Bayou channel comes through and the Fins & Feathers Marina is located, and where the Lydia Ann Channel meets the Corpus Christi Channel and the Aransas Chan-nel. Port Aransas Harbor offers marinas, ramps, and bait camps. Port Aransas itself is a resort town, with restaurants, shell and surf shops, and serious tackle shops. "Port A" is reached by road using the ferry from Harbor Island or taking State Highway 361 from Mustang Island.

South Bay, on the west side of the road from Aransas Pass, is very shallow and grassy in spots, with protruding marsh. To the north is deeper water and a channel from the Aransas Pass Municipal Harbor and Hampton's Landing. Several islands are close to the north shore, including Dagger Island. The merging with Corpus Christi Bay just across the Corpus Christi Channel is partially blocked by the marshy end of Mustang Island, Pelican Island, and an unnamed pair of islands across from Ingleside and cut by the ICW. A mild temperature range means win-ter fishing is good through most of the season, but the warmer months are best. Speckled trout and redfish are the big draws here, although a fisherman in 2007 caught a bull shark of more than 400 pounds in Aransa Bay near Lydia Ann Island and the ICW.

47 Corpus Christi Bay

Corpus Christi Bay is deep—10 to 14 feet on average. This means most open-bay fishing will be drifting or fishing under birds. The islands along the Corpus Chan-nel and spoil banks along the ICW offer some shallow-water opportunities, but the back shoreline of Mustang Island, like most such shorelines, is riddled with cuts, marshes, islands, and lakes.

Just inside the entrance to Corpus Christi Bay, on the western shore, is Oso Bay. The general rule that 90 percent of the fish are found in 10 percent of the water is true here—leave the open bay to sailboats, and fish the shorelines and grass beds. Coyote Island and several flats and grassy areas are just behind Port Aransas, in addition to Island Moorings Marina, which until recently was sanded in but is now listed as open to the bay again. There are several cuts leading to spots near the island shore and protected areas like Green Shack Cove and Pink Shack Cove, and Shamrock Cove behind Shamrock Island. Past Corpus is Nueces Bay, which runs almost to U.S. Highway 77 above Robstown.

Corpus Christi is a resort city in a large metropolitan setting. It lies on a beautiful bay, with a world-class municipal marina, museums, resort hotels, restaurants, and the Texas State Aquarium. From Corpus, US 77 leads to other adventures along the lower Texas coast, all the way to Brownsville in the semitropical Rio Grande Valley, which is located on about the same latitude as Key West, Florida.

The Laguna Madre

The Laguna Madre is the most unique bay system on the Gulf Coast. It only has three outlets to the Gulf—Port Aransas, the Port Mansfield cut through Padre Island, and the Brazos Santiago Pass at Brownsville—and this, combined with a very low freshwater influx due to few major streams flowing into the bay, makes it a hypersaline estuary, with a higher salt concentration than the Gulf of Mexico.

Most scientific data would indicate a poor fishery under such conditions, but the opposite is actually true. Even with the shallow water in the Laguna—just 2 to 5 feet in the Upper Laguna Madre—fishing for redfish, trout, and flounder is excellent, and some anglers also target big sheepshead in "holes" in the sea grass. The shallow water and hard sand bottom make this the top wade-fishing venue on the entire Gulf coast and a mecca for saltwater fly fishers, who target tailing reds on the shallow flats.

Because the ICW runs down the middle of most of the length of the Laguna Madre, access by boat is fairly easy, but road access is very limited. Between Corpus Christi and Baffin Bay, there are virtually no roads leading to the bay on the mainland, and the only vehicle travel down Padre Island is on the beach. This lack of access and development is an indication of another condition that is unique to Texas—extremely large family ranches that have seen no reason to sell their property to developers or corporate interests.

48 Baffin Bay and Upper Laguna Madre

The exception to the access situation is Baffin Bay, a fairly large and deep bay cutting inland from the Laguna Madre that offers some of the best speckled trout fishing on the Gulf. If any thought is given to the situation, it makes perfect sense. In an extremely shallow bay system, the deepest water—in this case, the ICW and Baffin Bay—will naturally attract a large proportion of the available fish, at least some of the time.

Baffin Bay is just below Kingsville, once known mostly as the headquarters city of the historic King Ranch. From Riviera on U.S. Highway 77, take State Highway 771 to Riviera Beach. Several bait camps and an RV park are located in this area, which is the upper end of Baffin, where the Laguna Salada splits to the west, Cayo del Grullo to the east. There is a boat ramp at the Seawind RV Resort, on County Road 114 west off SH 771 and a ramp at the nearby Kaufer-Hubert Memorial Park. The remainder of Baffin Bay is within the King Ranch boundaries, so there is no development from here to the Laguna.

In sharp contrast to the Laguna Madre, Baffin boasts 5- to 9-foot depths, and it also has a very unusual geological formation. There are huge underwater rocks in Baffin, mostly around midbay, with names such as Starvation Point Rocks, South Rocks, Center Rocks, White Bluff Rocks, and Windmill Rocks. *Big* speckled trout are taken around these rocks on topwater plugs and soft plastic baits, and the last

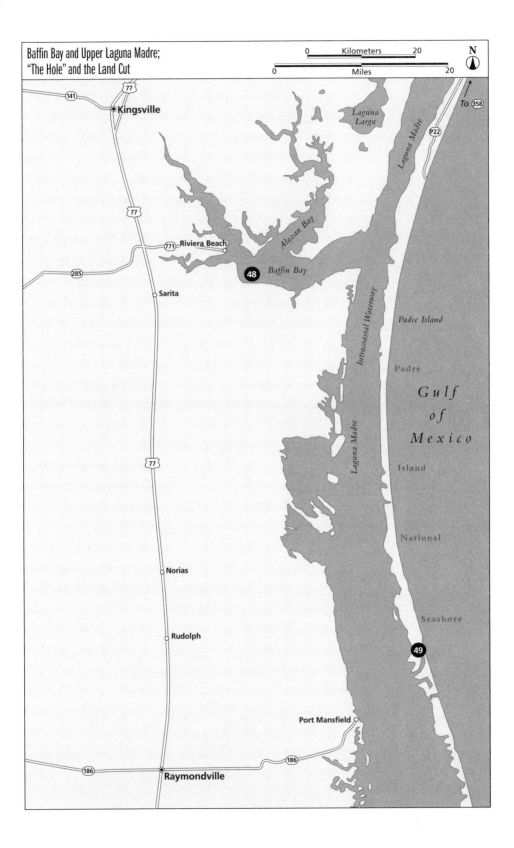

Baffin Bay and Upper Laguna Madre;
"The Hole" and the Land Cut

Kilometers 0 — 20
Miles 0 — 20

N

Kingsville

Laguna Larga

To 358

Riviera Beach

Alazan Bay

Baffin Bay

48

Sarita

Intracoastal Waterway

Padre Island

Padre

Gulf
of
Mexico

Island

Laguna Madre

National

Seashore

49

Norias

Rudolph

Port Mansfield

Raymondville

Texas state record trout was caught here on a fly rod. Boaters should be wary of the rocks, as many outboard lower units have paid the price for careless navigation.

Alazan Bay breaks off to the east around Starvation Point. It has one set of rocks, but mostly a soft mud bottom not suitable for wading. The main length of Baffin is a trout fisher's dream, with deep water in the center and wadeable flats along the shoreline. For anglers entering from the ICW, the cut is to the west of the bay's mouth. To the east is an area known as the Badlands, plus shallow flats. The actual entrance is narrow but has 7- to 9-foot depths.

The Upper Laguna Madre outside Baffin runs from shallow to very shallow, except for dredge areas just outside the ICW and the shoreline between the mouth of Baffin and the Land Cut. There are spoil islands along the ICW, plus a few platforms providing additional fishing structure. The Padre Island shoreline has cuts, islands, flats, and other prime wade-fishing areas. Speckled trout of trophy size are the big draw, and winter is perhaps the best time to fish for them here. Redfish and sheepshead will also be found around the rocks, and flounder in the shallow areas in spring and fall.

49 "The Hole" and the Land Cut

Many Texas maps show the Laguna Madre as one long bay, running from Corpus Christi Bay to Brownsville. The lack of major storms hitting this area and the limited water flow through this system have in recent years allowed serious sanding in of the Laguna below Baffin Bay, to the point that without the ICW, the island would sometimes not be an island at all. Seen from the air, it appears as though a large sandbar has crept across the Laguna from the Padre Island beach, jumped the ICW, and spread onto the mainland.

The spot where the ICW cuts through is known as the Land Cut because it originally left the bay and diverted through the mainland. Now it is the cut connecting the two bays, which makes it the only transit for fish seeking passage in either direction. This, coupled with the deeper water, makes it a prime fishing area, protected from high winds and without the constant barge traffic found in the ICW to the north. Although there are a few canals coming off the Main Canal where the ranch needed landings, again, there is no access by road in this part of the Laguna, and therefore no bait camps, boat ramps, or other facilities. The only way to reach the Land Cut is by a long boat ride.

The area between Padre Island and the Land Cut is very low and may not be dry land at all times. High tides can flood all or part of this section, possibly rejoining the Upper and Lower Laguna Madre. Should a major storm hit this area in the future, it could flush it out for several years.

A finger bay known as "The Hole" is the portion of the Laguna south of the Land Cut that is blocked off by the connecting bar. It is half the length of the entire Upper Laguna on a strong high tide and is very shallow, and while it could offer good fishing, the remote nature of this spot makes it an unwise choice for boaters not familiar with the immediate area. It is also known as "The Graveyard," by the way. The Land Cut also offers good winter fishing for trout and reds; spring through fall, add flounder to the mix. This is a little north for snook, but just barely.

50 Lower Laguna Madre

Immediately exiting the Land Cut is an island on the mainland side known as Rincon de San Jose. Trying to go behind it will introduce a boater to shallow mud flats, but good wading areas can be found on the bay side and on the north side of the ICW. The areas immediately outside the ICW are fairly deep, running to as much as 9 feet. There are many areas of sea grass, with good wade-fishing in the grass along the King Ranch shoreline.

One popular area just before the Mansfield Channel is known as Community Bar, and the water between there and the channel is known as Redfish Bay—for good reason. South of the ICW are several small islands, large grass beds, and a continuation of Community Bar. Several channels cut off from the ICW into the shallow portions of the bay, but the shoreline area off Padre Island is only a couple feet deep. Because this is a sanded-in area, it is without the coves and cuts found in the island to the north, but makes for a very pleasant wading area.

Drift fishing is a popular method nearer the ICW, but there are many uncharted rocks in this bay to watch out for. The spoil islands to the west of the Mansfield Channel present a barrier to travel down the bay—taking the ICW across is the safest route. Port Mansfield has a restaurant or two, a couple convenience stores, lodging, bait, fuel, boat ramps—everything but a grocery store. The area where the channel cuts through Padre Island offers fishing in the cut itself, wade fishing on the north island shoreline on either side, and excellent surf fishing on the Gulf side of the cut. The jetties also offer great fishing for many species not encountered to the north.

To the west of the ICW, very shallow water and spoil islands on the north side make this area unsuitable to fish except on a high tide. The other side of the ICW is no deeper, but this creates a shallow-water angler's paradise. Flats-feeding reds and trout know they have miles of territory to flee to, so they are not as skittish as would be expected in such an exposed environment. This bay is what the shallow-running boats are made for.

The ICW runs almost to the shore a bit farther down, allowing access to shore-line areas. This section of shoreline is not in the King or Kennedy Ranches; it is, however, in the Laguna Atascosa National Wildlife Refuge. The Arroyo Colorado Cutoff comes in from the Arroyo Colorado itself, a small river thought to have been an arm of the Rio Grande a long time ago. From U.S. Highway 77, at Combes, take County Road 508 to a right turn (south) onto State Highway 1420. Take a quick turn left (east) onto County Road 106 through Rio Hondo to a left (north) onto County Road 2925 to Arroyo City, where you will find a marina and the Adolph Thomas Jr. County Park, with boat ramps and other facilities. Just south is Rattle-snake Bay, where catches of snook are very possible.

The mainland side of the ICW has spoil islands, shoreline islands, and grass flats. Just past Stover Point the water depth increases to 4 to 5 feet, and roads off County Road 510 lead to launch spots at Laguna Vista and Holly Beach. State Highway 100 also leads into Port Isabel, across from the city of South Padre Island. The ICW basically ends just past the South Point Marina and Boatyard in Port Isabel, after a journey down the east coast of the United States, across the tip of Florida, and around the Gulf Coast.

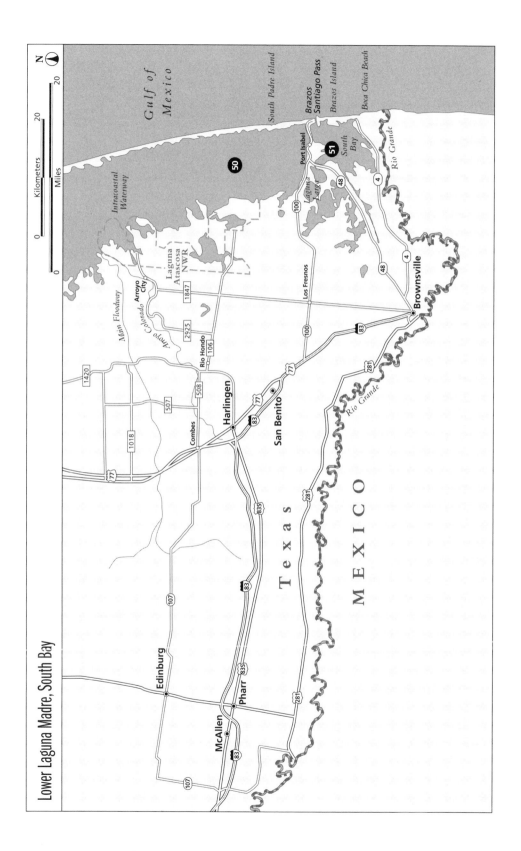

Lower Laguna Madre, South Bay

Port Isabel offers bait and boat ramps, along with city amenities. Fishing is good around the Queen Isabella Causeway, leading to South Padre Island, and in the bay between the island and the mainland. The bay side of South Padre Island has three fishing piers and launch ramps, in addition to three marinas. Because South Padre Island has the same latitude as Key West, Florida, fishing for warm-water species is pretty much a year-round activity, although there will be more sunshine from spring through fall. Besides the usual cast of characters like speckled trout, redfish, and flounder, here we have a reliable chance at snook in the back bay areas and tarpon at the jetties.

51 South Bay

Across the Brownsville Ship Channel is South Bay, which offers good wade fishing and a shortcut to Boca Chica Beach for shallow-draft boats. Although only a few feet deep and with no facilities of any kind—and on the side of a long lonely road to nearly nowhere—South Bay is important by virtue of its being the most southerly body of water on the Texas coast. South Bay is accessible almost exclusively from a cut in the Brownsville ship channel to boats launched from either Port Isabel or South Padre Island. This is one of the more dependable spots for snook. The link to the channel and Laguna Madre mean flounder and redfish will be here, also. Although the climate is temperate, north winds in winter can make South Bay too shallow to enter or fish; only very shallow draft boats or kayaks can float there under the best of conditions.

Here our journey that began on Sabine Lake at the Louisiana border comes to an end at the Mexican border. But while the trek down the coast is concluded, the fishing adventure has just begun!

The "World's Largest Flyrod" is located at the base of the Queen Isabella Causeway, leading from Port Isabel on the mainland to South Padre Island.

Near Offshore

Most coastal states claim only the waters 3 miles offshore from their beaches, leaving regulation of all the waters between this point and the 200-mile international limit to the federal government. Texas is different, in that our state retains ownership up to 9 nautical miles from the shoreline. This means that quite a bit of very productive fishing water falls under the jurisdiction of the state of Texas.

For most of the common fish species found in these waters, state regulations mirror those in federal waters, with the exception of red snapper, a popular and tasty species found around oil production platforms and underwater structure. National Oceanic and Atmospheric Administration (NOAA) Fisheries, the agency in charge of regulating both commercial and recreational fishing for saltwater species in federal waters, considers red snapper overfished and has instituted a closed season. In 2008 the closure lasted from September 30 until June 1. The season closed August 5 the next year. For several years the daily bag limit for snapper had been four fish per day in federal waters, but this was reduced by an "emergency rule" to a measly two fish per angler per day. Texas allows red snapper fishing year-round in state waters and is not likely to lower the four-fish limit.

While there is a limited population of red snapper in Texas waters, since it is mainly a deepwater, structure-oriented species, this difference in regulations does allow some leeway for Texas anglers in pursuit of snapper. Texas officials do not necessarily agree that snapper are in danger, and feel the western portion of the Gulf should be regulated differently than the rest of this body of water.

Fat red snapper can be caught in Texas offshore waters and are tasty eating. The top fish is 16 inches, minimum legal size in federal waters. The bottom snapper is a 15-inch "Texas Snapper."

Other near-offshore species found in "Texas" waters are more common. King and Spanish mackerel feed almost on the beach at times, and bonito—properly "little tunny"—roam inside Texas waters and are excellent light-tackle adversaries. Jack crevalle is one of the premier light-tackle species anywhere, and they may be found from the beach to the Texas offshore boundary. Ling, known as cobia elsewhere, are also targeted. When conditions are right, offshore species such as dolphin enter Texas waters, and it is not unheard of for sailfish to be caught within 5 miles or so of shore. Grouper can be found in Texas waters, especially in winter, but common Gulf species such as amberjack, tuna, and wahoo, along with many others, will require a bit longer boat ride.

Generally speaking, most of the water conditions and fish characteristics of near-offshore waters are consistent along the whole Texas coast—with a few notable exceptions.

Along the Surf Line

Many bay boats are capable of fishing the waters just off the beach in calm conditions and when the run from port is not very long, in the event bad weather should threaten. Surf-launched boats, however, of various types can provide access to nearshore waters far from normal Gulf outlets and passes.

In spring and again in fall, huge schools of mullet often raft in the breakers close to the beach, making them easy prey for marauding jacks and tarpon. Often, these fish will be well within casting range of surf and pier anglers, but other times they will remain just a little too far out, making a boat a necessary piece of equipment for their pursuit. Jacks are notoriously messy feeders, and there will usually be other fish following beneath to feast on the scraps, including bull reds, sharks, and big stingrays, in addition to smaller species. These feeding periods can repeat all day long, and the sight of a school of big jacks plowing through a school of mullet—causing them to shower into the air—is awe inspiring. Even more so is a huge silver tarpon blasting clear of the water and crashing back in, throwing white water high around it.

Live mullet are excellent bait in these situations, but fresh-cut mullet can be even better, since the pieces leak blood and juices and resemble what the jacks might leave. Actually, any sort of cut bait will draws strikes. Various lures, cast or trolled, are also good choices, especially big spoons and metal trolling plugs like Russell Lures or King Getters. Big swimming plugs also work.

Even when baitfish and feeding activity are not observed, predator species will usually be cruising the guts between sandbars and the water just beyond, as the bars are the main form of "structure" in this area of the Gulf. Trolling beyond the breakers covers a lot of water while looking for hungry fish. Another good technique is "chumming" with small bits of cut-up baitfish to attract predators to your boat. When chumming, cut bait may have an advantage over live bait, as long as it is fresh. Fish at least one bait weighted near the bottom, one suspended under a balloon or other float, and another drifted near the surface with no weight. Chumming from a mile to 7 miles from the beach can produce bull reds, stingrays, tarpon, jacks, big gafftop catfish, Spanish mackerel, and even king mackerel and lings.

Open Water

Past the breakers, the bottom of the Gulf off Texas is mostly a gradual, sandy slope, with very few nearshore reefs or other natural bottom structure. Here fish are found either when following schools of bait or while searching for them. Trolling open water is not as productive as fishing bait schools, but fish are caught.

When a school of feeding Spanish mackerel or bonito is found, stop the boat short of the school and chum if these resources are available, drift natural baits into the path of the school if the current allows, or cast appropriate artificials in front of and into the midst of the school. Popping rods are appropriate for this type of fishing, though heavier gear—at least 30-pound tackle—will be necessary for tarpon or sharks.

Oil Rigs

Texas is an oil-producing state as much as a cattle-producing one—maybe more so—and a lot of that oil comes from offshore wells. Many of these oil production platforms are close to shore and provide fish-attracting structure in areas of the Gulf where no natural structure exists. An oil rig is an artificial reef system that covers the entire water column from the surface to the bottom of the Gulf. This means that bottom feeders as well as surface species will be attracted to this structure. Red snapper can gravitate toward rigs amazingly close to shore, but close rigs get fished pretty hard, as one might expect, unless they are far down the beach from a Gulf outlet. Gulf trout are a more likely product of bait dropped to the bottom in less than 50 feet of water.

Migratory pelagic species, such as mackerel and ling, are thought to use the magnetic impulses from the steel in an oil rig for orientation and navigation, as well as feeding around the abundant baitfish attracted by a rig. Spanish mackerel and kings can be found at rigs very close in. My fishing companions and I once sat tied to a rig 12 miles off the beach but well down the coast from Freeport, where most boats were not likely to be fishing, and caught red snapper, king mackerel, and dolphin, and watched a decent wahoo swim around the platform several times. Nearly all rigs will have a population of triggerfish and spadefish around to steal baits intended for more desirable species, but both of these can be eaten—triggerfish are actually quite good—and they are very sporting adversaries on rod and reel.

A good technique for rig fishing is to troll to the platform and make a couple of passes around it. If your boat is equipped with a fish finder, check to see which side of the rig fish are gathered on. Normally this will be the down-current side, which is the best side to tie up to, with either a rig hook or a rope. After fishing a rig for some period of time and electing to leave, always troll around it one or two times—bait in the water and chum may have attracted fish that have not yet made it to your baits. Drifting a rig can be very productive. Work the sides the current flows past, floating with the current or wind, whichever is stronger, and use unweighted baits or a jig and bait trailer.

The deeper the water the rig sits in, the better the fishing, generally speaking. At the limit of Texas waters, the depth might be from 25 to 55 feet, depending on what part of the coast the rig is located off of. Water depth increases from the upper coast to the lower coast. Rigs are marked on most charts, and the close ones we are dealing with here can be seen from the beach on a clear day, so exotic navigational instruments and skills are not usually required to locate them. Occasionally the crew on a manned rig will ask that anglers not tie up, and fishers should always move away from a rig when a service boat pulls up. Be careful to not get too close to a structure, especially the up current side, and not to drift too close. Steel trumps fiberglass in the event of a boat-rig collision.

Wrecks

A form of structure that increases over the years comes from wrecks. Some large vessels have been purposely sunk by the government to create fish-attracting structure, such as the *George Vancouver* Liberty Ship which sank about 4 miles off Bryan Beach, near Freeport, as it was being towed to a preferred spot farther offshore. Other wrecks include pleasure boats that have accidentally sunk.

The most common wrecks are the remains of shrimp boats sunk by bad weather or the deteriorating condition of the vessel itself. Because shrimping bycatch is known to be detrimental to the welfare of many fish species, it is almost poetic justice that sunken shrimp boats provide needed structure to give food and shelter to many of these same species. A good way to think of this is that every old wooden shrimp boat out there fishing is a snapper reef looking for a place to happen.

Sunken boats in the area ranging from just off the beach to 9 miles out are home to bottom species like red snapper and Gulf trout, and often a grouper or two. Mackerel will feed around and over wrecks, as will tarpon, lings, jacks, and sharks. Triggerfish are certain to be over any wreck, just as they are found around all oil rigs.

Natural Structure

Many people think the bottom of the Gulf from the shore to many miles out is a mud and sand desert, with no natural structure to hold fish in areas where there are no rigs, large valves on oil pipelines, or wrecks. This is not entirely true. Beginning at Freeport, with the offshore ridge made up of the East Bank, Middle Bank, and Shell Ridge, there are elevated sections of bottom interspersed with deeper holes that attract and hold several types of fish. Moving farther down the coast, there are more areas like this not far off the Texas shoreline.

The most notable of this type of formation occurs farther south, off Padre Island and the mouth of the Rio Grande. Entering the Gulf through the Mansfield Cut that separates North and South Padre Island, there are rocks in 40 to 90 feet of water as close as 5 miles from land that harbor excellent snapper fishing year-round. This structure also attracts marauding king mackerel and other species. The rock pile off the mouth of the Rio Grande, which local legend says was created by floodwaters carrying off material from the construction of the Brownsville jetties (does this make it an artificial reef?), is credited for the variety of offshore species sometimes caught around the jetties or in the water just beyond them.

Watch the Surf

Finally, there is the surf itself as fish-attracting structure. The sand bars formed by centuries of pounding waves and the guts between them attract game fish and bait species. So do the waves themselves, which provide cover for large fish feeding in the shallow water.

It was long assumed that bull reds came to the surf to spawn, hoping that incoming tides would carry their eggs through the passes and into the back bays. It seems much more likely that reds spawn in deeper water offshore, and the young swim inshore under their own power. What the big reds come to the surf for, then, is most likely to feed on bait confused and disoriented in the crashing waves.

Special Places

Any coastline is special. Where the oceans and land mass meet is an ecosystem unlike any other, and in this book we have dealt with the various stages of this place of transitions between the liquid and solid worlds—the nearshore Gulf, the surf line, and the bays and tidal streams. There will, however, always be certain places that stand out as being extra special even in such a unique environment.

Since the Texas coast is longer than most, it might be expected to have a good number of those special places. I have my own selection of these spots, garnered from thirty-seven years of sampling as much of the Gulf shoreline as possible. I have saved the best for last.

Not everyone will share my list—there are other places that people classify as special due to their own memories, experiences, and preferences. Baffin Bay, for instance, would be on most lists but is not on mine because I am not an ardent inshore fisherman. Padre Island is one of the most special spots on any coast, but it is not on my list because it is so obvious. My preference for special places, the ones I'd like to share with you, is for spots a little less publicized. Some of these are a bit remote and hard to reach, and some can be driven to on your way somewhere else. Give them a try the first chance you get.

52 High Island

The beach around and above the actual town of High Island is special because it is normally less crowded than Galveston and other areas close to large cities. There are still more anglers on this beach than surfers and sand-castle-building contestants. The piers close to High Island provide good fishing, but I have caught bull reds off the beach between them. The beach to the north can be a bit difficult to drive on because of a clay layer beneath the sand—which can sometimes be felt when wading out to cast—but the wreckage of Highway 87 can be used to get to more remote spots. Legally, this road is posted as closed between Sabine Pass and High Island, but you might see an eighteen-wheeler barreling past the barricade on the south end.

The really good news about High Island is that the angle of the shoreline—or maybe some other factor, like the slope of the bottom as it slides into the Gulf—keeps the waves calmer and smaller than on the lower portions of the Texas shoreline. Calm surf might be bad for long boarders, but it is good for those wishing to wade past the second bar with a surf rod or to ferry a shark bait past the bars in a surf-launched boat.

While the surf at High Island is often calmer than in spots farther south and west, the water is generally not as clear. The bottom from the beach to the first sandbar can be sticky clay, with sharp rocks in some spots.

The really bad news is that the mosquitoes on this section of the coast are terrible. All the "land" fronting the beach is mostly salt marsh, a wonderful breeding ground for these creatures but one that does not allow them many feeding opportunities, save for a few sad cattle and fishers minding their own business on the beach! I have fished High Island in the winds of an approaching hurricane, standing in the lee of a smoky driftwood fire, and had the little vampires bite me

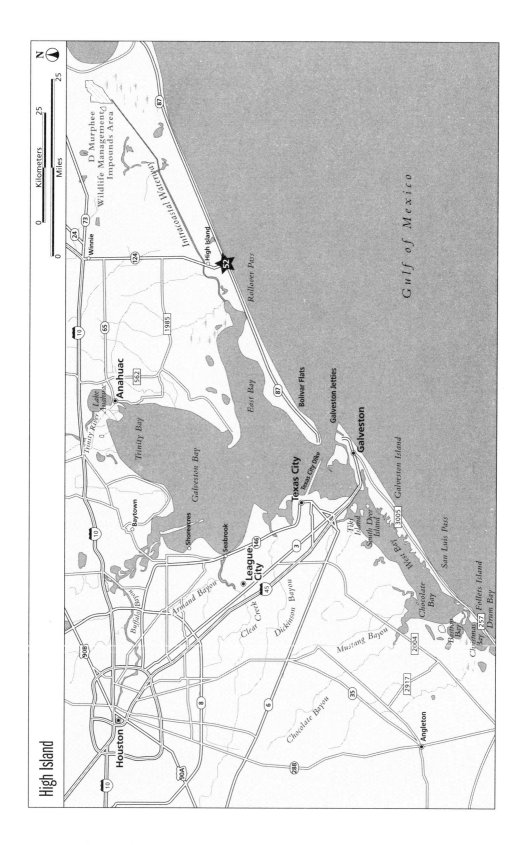

High Island

N

Kilometers
0   25   25
Miles
0   25

Houston

90A
10
8
908
10
24
73
Winnie
D Murphee
Wildlife Management
Impounds Area
65
10
562
Anahuac
Lake Anahuac
Trinity River
Trinity Bay
Baytown
Buffalo Bayou
Armand Bayou
Clear Creek
Dickinson Bayou
Mustang Bayou
Chocolate Bayou
288
6
35
2917
2004
Angleton
257
Drum Bay
Christmas Bay
Bastrop Bay
Follets Island
San Luis Pass
Chocolate Bay
West Bay
3005
Galveston Island
South Deer Island
Tiki Island
3
146
45
League City
Seabrook
Shoreacres
Galveston Bay
Texas City
Texas City Dike
Galveston
Galveston Jetties
Bolivar Flats
East Bay
87
1985
124
High Island
52
Rollover Pass
Intracoastal Waterway
87

Gulf of Mexico

through heavy clothes on my downwind side. They are much worse at night, when beach fishing for big fish like sharks and reds is best. In the daytime, the mosquitoes are replaced by horseflies that dive bomb, bite off a painful mouthful of flesh, and buzz off before you even see them coming. I have heard in recent years that nudists have found portions of this beach to their liking. They must have found a very good bug repellant!

Despite these drawbacks, fishing can be excellent for bull reds, shark, black drum, jack crevalles, speckled trout, panfish—even tarpon—and other species. Spring though fall is the peak time to surf fish High Island, although many people enjoy this beach in winter for birding and beach walking, when the bugs are not quite as bad.

There are two good fishing piers along this portion of beach; a third close to High Island was destroyed by a hurricane many years ago. Mecom's Pier is closest to High Island; the Dirty Pelican Pier is farther down the beach. Both offer access to deeper water by anglers on foot for a nominal fee.

Along most of the Texas coast where the road parallels the beach, there will be beach access points cut through the dunes. Some are paved, while others are just sand—these are to be used with caution, as they are often traps for two-wheel-drive vehicles.

Another problem that can arise here for those who run baits out for big sharks or to reach reds holding farther out is that shrimpers may pull their nets over your baited hooks. When this happens, you will be in for a fight you cannot win. On most beaches where small shrimp boats work the surf, nighttime is safe for deep fishing, as it is illegal to shrimp the surf at night in Texas, but here the locals sometimes forget that.

Despite the insects and shrimp boats, or perhaps because of them, fishing pressure is lighter, and the fishing can be very good. I remember awaking one morning after fighting bugs all night to see mullet being chased by big jack crevalles in flat, calm surf very close in. I hastily cast-netted two live mullet, baited a rod, and immediately got a smashing hit from a 20-pound-class jack. After fighting and landing the jack, I grabbed a second rod and bait, cast out again, and caught another fish almost the same size. Two baits, two casts, two hard-fighting jacks—too much fun! On another very similar morning, I opened my eyes to see a school of bull reds "tailing"—that is, feeding with heads down and tails extending above the surface of the water—in the first shallow gut off the beach. This remains the only time I have seen reds so large in water so small.

Even though the High Island surf is not usually as clear as the water farther down the coast, tarpon—a species generally associated with clear water—are often seen smashing bait beyond casting range of the beach, and they have been hooked here off the piers. Tarpon guides from Galveston make the run down the shoreline by boat to fish off High Island in the calm weather of late summer and find good numbers of silver kings. It is common to see the big "pogy boats"—fishing ships that launch smaller chase boats to surround massive schools of menhaden (called "pogies" in Louisiana)—with nets working just closer than the horizon, indicating large concentrations of baitfish are present. These vessels come from Louisiana, around the port of Cameron, where a processing plant is located. All the small game fish and panfish species found in the surf elsewhere in Texas are caught at High Island.

High Island itself is a small town with a few shell shops, net shops to repair shrimp nets, and a basic but nice motel with a good restaurant. There are bait, groceries, gasoline, and other services available. High Island has a school system that attracts quality teachers by offering them free lodging in homes owned by the city. For a short stay—or longer visit, if you can put up with the bugs—this can be a pleasant and restful place to waste some time.

Driving, parking, and camping on the beach are legal, and the time-honored beach campfire is still permissible here. It is possible to drive on the beach all the way to Rollover Pass, halfway down the Bolivar Peninsula, but this should only be attempted in a four-wheel-drive vehicle. Bolivar separates East Bay from the Gulf of Mexico, and drivers down Highway 87 can glance to the north and often see tugboats pushing barges in the ICW, which runs down the edge of the peninsula.

High Island can be reached by taking Highway 73 west from Port Arthur or Interstate 10 east from Beaumont to the town of Winnie, then taking Highway 124 to High Island. Or drive up the Bolivar Peninsula on Highway 87 from Galveston. The town was so-named because it is built on the only high ground in a vast stretch of coastal marsh. Highway 87 and the beach can be picked up just past the city limits.

53 Wolf Island

On the other side of the Brazos River is an island known as "Wolf Island," bounded by the Gulf, the Brazos and San Bernard Rivers, and the Intracoastal Waterway (ICW). There are no bridges to this small island, nor any ferries. The only access is by boat due to the Cedar Lake cuts through the beach between here and Sargent.

Thus, there is no vehicular traffic on the Wolf Island beach, which is often too covered with driftwood logs that came down the Brazos to be driven on anyway. Sometimes it is even possible to walk long distances on wood without ever touching the sand.

The lack of vehicular beach traffic means fish—often big fish—are not afraid to feed close to shore, and the almost total lack of fishing pressure means hardly anyone is there to catch them when they do come in. This is an excellent spot to surf fish for bull reds, tarpon, and large sharks, and schools of smaller fish, like speckled trout, can often be found chasing bait just off the beach on calm days. Early spring through late fall provides a long window to visit and fish Wolf Island, and exploration in winter will see less of the bugs and snakes.

The same current that brings sand from up the coast to the mouth of the San Bernard River scours the surf guts a little deeper here. Bull reds are the most obvious reason to run a boat across the Brazos or down the San Bernard. The big breeders will be feeding in the first gut at times, where they can be challenged with either live bait or artificial lures—big ones—on light tackle for exceptional sport.

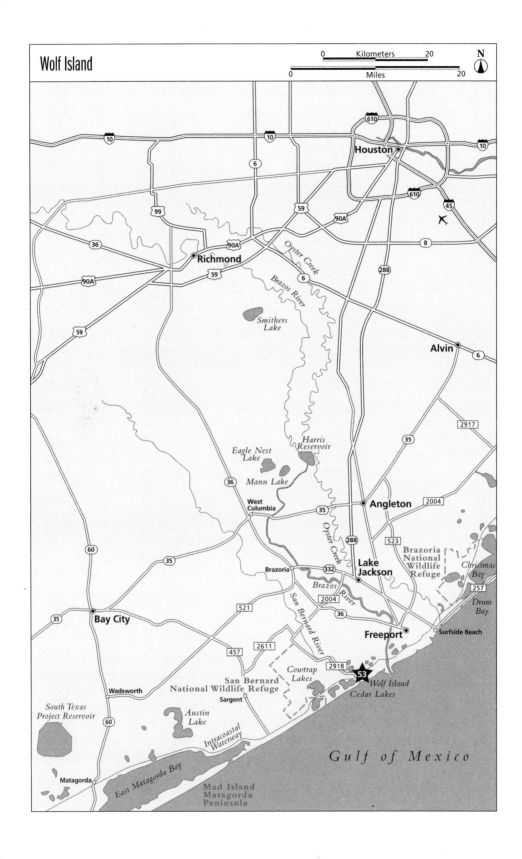

Wolf Island

0   Kilometers   20

0   Miles   20

N

Houston

Richmond

Alvin

Oyster Creek

Brazos River

Smithers Lake

Harris Reservoir

Eagle Nest Lake

Mann Lake

West Columbia

Angleton

Oyster Creek

Lake Jackson

Brazoria

Brazos River

Brazos

San Bernard River

Bay City

Wadsworth

Sargent

San Bernard National Wildlife Refuge

Cowtrap Lakes

Wolf Island
Cedar Lakes

Freeport

Surfside Beach

Brazoria National Wildlife Refuge

Christmas Bay

Drum Bay

South Texas Project Reservoir

Austin Lake

Intracoastal Waterway

Matagorda

East Matagorda Bay

Mad Island
Matagorda Peninsula

Gulf of Mexico

53

The channel through the surf from the Brazos once ran in the gut between the second and third sandbars, but in the last decade this gut has been washed out into a large "lagoon," and the offshore sandbar is now exposed above the surf on all but the highest tides. This should make for a very interesting fishing spot for those using a seaworthy but shallow-draft craft—like a good rigid-hull inflatable—to access and explore here.

The mouth of the San Bernard River is a subject of concern as I write this, as it is sanded almost completely closed. Residents blame the Army Corps of Engineers for rerouting the Brazos all those years ago, saying the sand washing from Surfside Beach and the "New" Brazos mouth has shut off the river's route to the Gulf. The Corps of Engineers has decided to open the river mouth with a dredged channel 10 feet deep. Work was scheduled to begin in fall of 2008.

The mouth can now be reached only by boat, and although having the river closed affects the dynamics of coastal tidal flow down the beach and through the ICW, it also creates another, though rather small, section of undisturbed beach to fish for those who make the effort to reach it. Technically, it is possible to drive the beach to the San Bernard from Sargent in a heavy-duty four-wheel drive or some sort of ATV, but expect new cuts to open from the several small lakes that make up the Cedar Lakes on both sides of the ICW as the river current looks for a new path to the Gulf.

When there was an active shark-fishing club in Brazoria County, its members gathered most often at the mouth of the Brazos to fish, but they also made regular trips onto Wolf Island both to fish and to seine for bait. Small tarpon were frequently taken in the net. In those days, the channel coming out of the river veered to the west through the second gut off the beach. Using caution, a small boat such as a johnboat loaded with gear could cross the river and run a good distance down the gut, then be pulled by wading fishers just about as far down the beach as they wished to fish.

Near the end of the river's run along the surf is the cut through the beach to Lost Lake, a large, shallow area that could be floated with a shallow-draft boat, especially a kayak. Local legend has it that redfish are plentiful in Lost Lake, and there is no reason for them not to be. A section of the "Old Intracoastal" canal cuts into the island behind Lost Lake from the San Bernard and runs nearly to the Brazos. Ranchers run cattle on the island and have used the canal to load them onto barges. Anglers could use it to access the interior of the island, but it is mostly a marshy area highly populated by rattlesnakes.

Storms and erosion have drifted more sand to the edge of the Brazos River's influence and created a low-tide finger of dry sand that curves back to the Lost Lake opening, creating a much larger "lagoon" than was here twenty years ago. The water depth in this extra-large gut has not been confirmed, but it could possibly be a very good spot to tarpon fish, as the Brazos was once famous for tarpon activity well up the river, before industrial pollution chased them out for many years. A large lagoon bounded by a bar protruding above the water would concentrate bait and attract tarpon that come from the Gulf to feed in the river mouth.

Tarpon still roam the beachfront along Wolf Island, where they may be intercepted by a long cast from a surf rod or by boaters either launching a small craft in the river or making the run from the Freeport jetties. Big sharks are still here, too, and might even be hooked in the daylight hours. Speckled trout roam the lagoon and the rivers, and flounder should also be numerous in the lake. Be careful wading across the entrance to Lost Lake during blue crab spawning season. I tried once and was almost eaten alive. Of course, the presence of so many crabs is also a good indicator of game fish—especially big reds and tarpon.

Anglers with a sense of adventure and an ability to "rough it" a bit can cross the rivers and camp on the beach. You'll have to take everything you might need with you, and plenty of it—including water and first-aid supplies. There are no restrictions on campfires and plenty of wood to build them with. Take tackle suited to both big game and small, as well as a good cast net to catch plenty of bait. You will be just as isolated, for practical purposes, as you would be at Big Shell on Padre Island—maybe more so, because not even a four-wheel-drive vehicle can interrupt your fishing. It can definitely be a worthwhile experience.

Anyone venturing to this or other hard-to-reach sections of Texas beach should be prepared with a cell phone, flares, first-aid equipment, and sufficient food and water. Never, ever attempt to swim across one of these rivers near its mouth.

There has not been a reliable source of bait along the San Bernard for many years. No road exists on the east bank of the river, but FM 2918 goes to River's End, on the ICW across from the approach to the mouth (where there is a boat ramp), from FM 2611 at Churchill. Boats can be launched at the Highway 36 ramp on the Brazos or from the beach at the river mouth.

54 Brown Cedar Cut

Brown Cedar Cut, named for the small windblown trees that serve as landmarks, has had an open-shut existence for a long time. Hurricanes blow it open, it sands back in, and another storm blows it open again. Before the new cut was made at Sargent, it was possible to drive the beach to the east side of the cut, when it was a cut. Brown Cedar has been closed so long and was such an outstanding fishing spot when it was open, that efforts were made to have it opened by the U.S. Army Corps of Engineers in the past, and one large construction company even proposed doing it for free.

When the cut was open, currents coming in and out from the Gulf provided excellent fishing for speckled trout and redfish, both in the surf and in the bay surrounding the area where the cut came in. Because Brown Cedar has been closed for so long, fishing pressure is now much lighter. Those seeking a quiet place to camp and fish could do much worse. Children can play on the beach here without nearly as much chance of being run over by a speeding car, and anglers might wade either side of the cut by day, switching with the incoming or outgoing tides, and set up long rods at night to challenge bull reds and sharks. Ospreys fly overhead, coyotes are seen sneaking through the dunes, and occasionally a white-tailed deer will make an appearance.

Brown Cedar Cut, Palacios

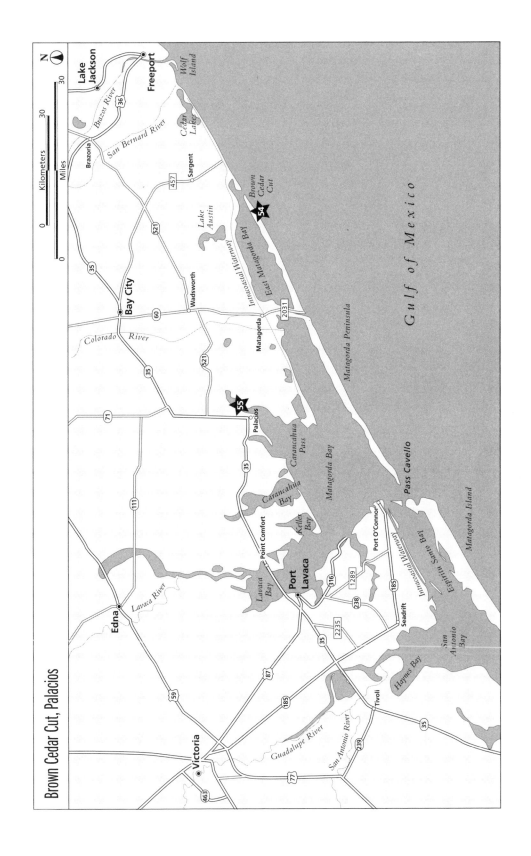

An expedition to Brown Cedar should begin with a list of necessities, including provisions and first-aid supplies. File a "float plan" letting someone know where you are going. Cell phones have made such trips safer than in the "old days"—just make sure yours is well charged, that a 12-volt accessory charger is available, and that your provider's service reaches here. Take a cast net to catch bait and plenty of ice to keep your catch and drinks cool.

Brown Cedar is remote in many ways, but not out of reach by any means. It can be a memorable trip on a reasonable budget that just about anyone can afford. The best chance of avoiding a crowd will come in early spring and late fall, which is luckily when the best fishing will be found here.

To get to Brown Cedar Cut, which really isn't a cut at the moment, you must drive up the beach on the Matagorda Peninsula from the mouth of the Colorado River below the town of Matagorda, something best accomplished in a four-wheel-drive vehicle. Alternately, you could get in a boat at Sargent and approach from the East Matagorda Bay side.

55 Palacios

Unlike Wolf Island or Brown Cedar, Palacios is right on Highway 35, between Bay City and Port Lavaca, so anyone can drive to it in any type of vehicle. There is also an airfield where those who fly can land their craft. With all its accessibility, however, Palacios is often overlooked by anglers and other visitors, to the point that its chamber of commerce refers to the city as the "Best-Kept Secret on the Texas Coast."

Fishing from the T head of the Palacios community pier.

FISHING THE TEXAS GULF COAST

Palacios is just over an hour's drive from Freeport, taking Highway 36 to Brazoria, then cutting west on FM 521 through Wadsworth (crossing Highway 60) to join Highway 35 only a few miles from the Palacios city limits. On the other hand, you can follow Highway 35 from Bay City to Palacios, a bit longer journey. As in most small towns along its route, Highway 35 either goes through the business section of town or skirts the outside edge of the city. Crossing Business 35 to the south, drive to South Bay Boulevard, which follows the bay shore for its entire length.

Palacios is on Tres Palacios Bay, which is fed by the Tres Palacios River and has the shallower Turtle Bay on its west side and Coon Bay on its east. The Palacios Ship Channel runs from the city across Matagorda Bay to the ICW, but even Tres Palacios Bay from the South Bay side out runs 3 to 7 feet deep. On the East Bay side, the water is much shallower. Most of the shoreline of Tres Palacios is oyster reefs, which are fish magnets. For whatever reason, Palacios is not as popular with outside anglers as Port O'Connor to the south, even though the fishing opportunities are very good. This is possibly because the wade fishing opportunities are not as numerous.

The Matagorda County Navigation District operates an excellent marina on the South Bay shoreline, but it is for members only. It offers open slips for larger vessels and covered slips with lifts for trailerable boats. Transient vessels can make arrangements for a temporary slip, and fuel is available. There is also a marina at the Serendipity RV Park on South Bay, and the municipal shrimp boat harbor, besides supporting the largest shrimping fleet on the Texas coast, also has some recreational boat slips and a protected boat ramp.

Tres Palacios Bay was supposedly named by crew members of one of the French explorer Robert de La Salle's vessels, which shipwrecked on a reef in Matagorda Bay. Swimming toward shore, they saw the mirage of three palaces before them. Although the mirage was gone when they got to land, the name stuck. The remains of the ship were excavated several years ago and will be displayed in a museum setting. The city holds an annual reenactment of La Salle's landing each July Fourth.

Palacios has invested a lot of money, much of it federal and state funds, to revitalize the bayfront. A paved walkway along the bayfront on South Bay connects a large number of smooth-surfaced rock groins and several longer wooden piers, all open to free public access and lighted at night. There are several boat ramps on both South and East Bays, but the best is on South Bay near South Point Marina. It is protected by a solid breakwater and has a large parking lot. A boatyard with haul-out capabilities is next door to the marina. Past Serendipity is the municipal shrimp-boat harbor, and farther down a teaching unit of Texas A&M University, and then the site of the old army base. Several parks with lovely landscaping are just off the bayfront. The Outrigger Restaurant serves excellent seafood, and on weekend nights Texas musicians perform live.

The Community Pier on South Bay extends well into the bay and is built on a fish-attracting oyster reef. There is a T head at the end for anglers, though speckled trout are caught toward shore as well. A wooden pavilion on the east side once held a seafood restaurant and concert area, but has been destroyed by hurricanes several times. The town is currently rebuilding it with grant money to hold events there again. Low tides will show more oyster reefs along the shoreline, as Tres Palacios Bay is well populated by these shellfish, and this makes it an excellent fishing area.

The Luther Hotel is the town's most noted landmark. Built in 1907 on the East Bay side, it was moved the next year using mules and wagons—and this is a three-story building stretching the length of a football field. When the army base was in operation, entertainers the likes of Rita Hayworth stayed there, and many prominent state and national politicians have visited as well. Best of all, the Luther is still open for business, behind an oleander-lined section of South Bay Avenue. The penthouse suite where Rita Hayworth stayed is still available for guests and is a very interesting room with a balcony looking out over the bay.

The homes along the bayfront are mostly old, large, and of Victorian architecture. Many are several stories high, with a "widow's walk" balcony around the second floor. Most have been restored, and a few are operated as bed-and-breakfasts. There are huge palm trees in the yards and a relaxed, Old South atmosphere all along the street. Several RV parks cater to winter Texans, and facilities are in place to offer aid to senior citizens.

Once outside of Tres Palacios Bay, anglers launching from Palacios can follow the ship channel across Matagorda Bay, but as this bay runs 12 to 14 feet deep with very few reefs, there is no reason to have to stay in the channel. This deep water can be drifted, or action may be found under birds working bait. The shoreline on both sides is lined with oysters, and the only large reef, Halfmoon, is to the east where

The pavilion on the Palacios Community pier.

the ICW enters Matagorda Bay. Crossing to the shoreline of Matagorda Peninsula gives access to a shallow shelf bordering a deep drop-off, and since the peninsula is actually an island, there is no vehicular traffic to frighten fish away.

The run to the ICW just below Port O'Connor is approximately 17 miles, and a few more miles put the boater through the Port O'Connor "big jetties" and into the Gulf. This channel is a bit tricky, as the current running through it is at times so strong that single-engine shrimp boats often cannot make way against it. When a strong outgoing tide is mated with a brisk southeast wind, it can be dangerous for small boats to traverse the channel in either direction. What this means is you pick your days, and only head offshore in very good weather.

Offshore of Port O'Connor, the water depth drops more quickly than to the north, and areas such as the East Breaks, 50 miles offshore, are prime billfish spots. King mackerel and other offshore species can often be caught just off the jetties, and red snapper fishing at rigs in state waters can be very good.

Inshore anglers leaving Palacios can fish many of the same spots anglers from Port O'Connor frequent, but with a shorter drive from areas like Houston and with much smaller crowds to deal with at the town's many boat ramps. Almost everything in Palacios will be less expensive than in Port O'Connor, from room rates to boat slip rental, because of less demand. Since the infrastructure is already in place to handle more crowds than currently frequent Palacios, and the city government is geared to increase the number of visitors, it will probably not remain a secret for much longer. Enjoy it while you can. The oyster reefs in the bay attract and hold speckled trout and reds all year, and the deep water of the bay should make this a non-stop fishing destination, weather permitting.

The historic Luther Hotel in Palacios was originally constructed in 1907.

56 Port Mansfield

Places at the end of a long road going nowhere else are always special. When that spot is more than just a jumping-off point to some of the best inshore and offshore fishing the Texas coast has to offer, it becomes even more so. Approximately 24 miles after leaving U.S. Highway 77 at Raymondville and turning east on Highway 186, Port Mansfield is surrounded by the famous King Ranch. Until recently land could only be leased from the ranch, not owned outright, and the King family has effectively kept development to a minimum, with industrialization not allowed at all.

Port Mansfield has a couple motels and fishing lodges, and a restaurant/bar or two, but no grocery store at the moment. There are two RV parks, a good boat ramp, and a marina with both covered slips and an open charter-boat dock. Expensive houses and town homes can be found here, as well as simple fishing cabins. The homes on the north side of town along the Laguna Madre have piers built out almost to the ICW, and there is a county park with a lighted pier at the very end of town. Many of the houses here are available as vacation rentals.

The ICW runs just off the shoreline as it passes Port Mansfield, offering access to fishing in the shallow Laguna both to the north and to the south. As it crosses the Laguna, the channel runs through great flats-fishing areas, and it allows the quickest reach to Padre Island anywhere—as long as you have a boat.

If world-class skinny-water fishing for reds and trout is not enough for your tastes, the offshore fishing out of Mansfield may satisfy you. Not only does the water drop off faster than along the upper coast, but there are also fish-holding

The county-owned marina at Port Mansfield has covered boat slips and a charter-boat dock.

FISHING THE TEXAS GULF COAST

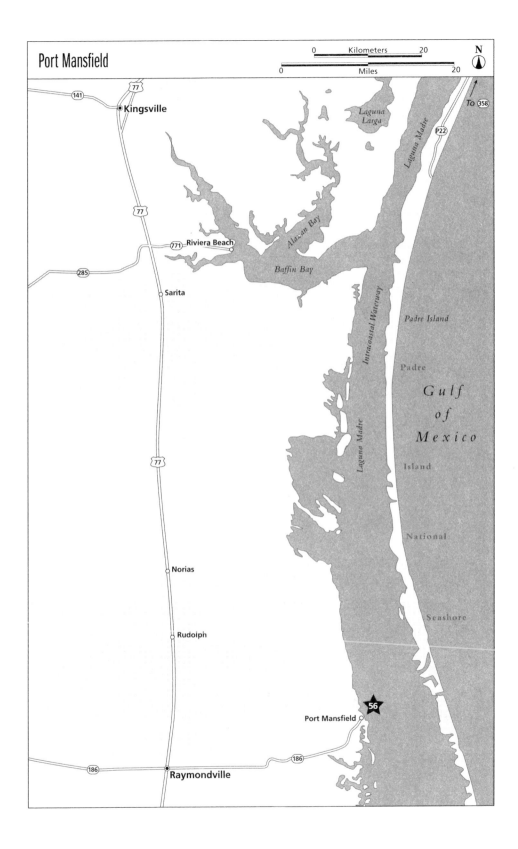

Port Mansfield

Kilometers 0 — 20
Miles 0 — 20

N

141
77
Kingsville
77
771 Riviera Beach
285
Sarita
77
Norias
Rudolph
Port Mansfield
186
186
Raymondville

Laguna Larga
Laguna Madre
To 358
P22
Alazan Bay
Baffin Bay
Intracoastal Waterway
Padre Island
Padre
Gulf
o f
Mexico
Island
Laguna Madre
National
Seashore

56

"rocks" not far offshore. Port Mansfield is one of the few places on the Texas coast where red snapper fishing is not just good inside state waters, but excellent. The most productive rocks lie within 5 miles of the island, in 60 to 90 feet of water, with charter captains reporting regular limits of 8- to 10-pound snapper on half-day outings. In warm weather, hordes of king mackerel roam close to shore, and during periods of extremely clear water, sailfish are sometimes hooked just off the jetties. Snook and tarpon are also encountered around the jetties with regularity. Big sharks feed along the surf and just offshore, too.

For serious offshore anglers, Port Mansfield can be the launch site for expeditions into the deeper Gulf for tuna, wahoo, big dolphins, and huge marlins. A state record yellowfin tuna was landed here, as well as a record blue marlin and dogtooth snapper.

Large party boats do not dock at Port Mansfield, nor do many big sportfishing yachts, due to the narrow channel across the bay, which has been subject to sanding in recent years. Most private and charter boats are less than 40 feet, and open center consoles are favored by many skippers. There is no boatyard operating at the time of this writing, so large boats requiring haul-outs for bottom jobs and routine or emergency maintenance must run either 70-plus miles to Port Aransas or 31 miles to Port Isabel.

Bay anglers use shallow-draft boats, mostly the "scooter" type, since the water in the Laguna Madre is only a foot or so deep in most places. Wade fishing requires a boat to get more than a short distance from the shoreline, due to the close proximity of the ICW.

The public county pier at Port Mansfield reaches within a long cast of the ICW and is lighted at night.

Visitors who rent a bayfront house with a lighted pier might not even care to go out in a boat, and certainly would not need to in order to catch fish. A decent cast from the end of most of the piers will land a bait near the ICW channel, and fishing under the lights for trout at night certainly beats absorbing the heat of the Texas sun in August. The public pier provides the same option as private ones, just without the guarantee of uncrowded conditions, as this is a popular spot for Raymondville residents to fish.

Mansfield is a very good place to launch an expedition to the isolated end of North Padre Island, since shallow-draft boats may be beached on the bay side, where a short hike takes you to the Gulf beach. Surf fishing here is excellent, and there are always the jetties to get your bait a bit farther out. Of course, the same precautions should be followed here as when venturing to any hard-to-reach spot on the coast—float plan, supplies, communication, and first-aid kit. Whether making the crossing for just a day trip or to camp on either side of the island for a while, this can be a very pleasant journey.

Because it is so isolated and public hunting is not allowed on the King Ranch land surrounding it, wild game is numerous around—and even in—Port Mansfield. Residents have stationed game feeders on the edge of town, and each evening folks gather or drive by to watch the show. White-tailed deer are plentiful and almost tame, grazing and relaxing in the front yards of homes facing the open land to the west of town.

On my last visit, I saw four deer grazing around a parked truck, while across the road a dozen fat wild turkeys roamed near the feeders. Javalinas, or collared peccaries, a small hoglike critter, also visit, and coyote sightings are not at all uncommon. While maybe not as exciting as the sundown show the jugglers and fire eaters put on in Key West, it is a much more laid-back and wholesome display—which is also a good definition of Port Mansfield in general. Because of the mild weather and almost tropical potential of fishing here, any time the wind isn't blowing too hard to safely take a boat out is a good time to fish for something. On sunny winter days, reds will be feeding on the flats, and speckled trout should be under the pier lights most nights. Winter snapper fishing at the close rocks is excellent, although the migratory pelagics like mackerel and sailfish will be gone for the coolest weather of the winter.

57 Boca Chica

Taking FM 4 east from Brownsville for 24 miles will lead a visitor to the stretch of beach between the south Port Isabel/Brownsville jetties and the mouth of the Rio Grande. While listed on maps as "Boca Chica" as though there were a town or village there, in reality it is just a 15-mile piece of empty beach—no stores, gas stations, or bait camps. There are a few fishers' cabins on stilts, but that's about it.

Turning north from FM 4 on the beach and traveling less than 10 miles brings us to the jetty, one of the most unique fishing spots for a boatless angler that I have ever experienced. One afternoon on my first trip to the Boca Chica region, I cast spoons on light tackle off the jetty into the channel and caught a mixed bag of sand

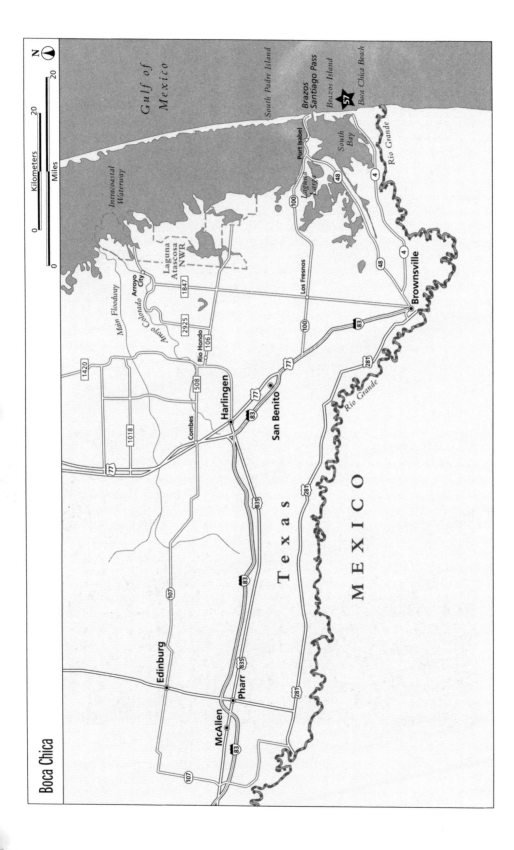

Boca Chica

trout and small groupers. That night on the beach, my surf rod bait was attacked by a huge school of large bluefish. This trip was in February—just a journey south to search for warm weather—so fishing opportunities had not yet "heated up," but the potential was obvious. The next morning I saw a tourist fishing the channel side of the jetty, catching small red snapper on light tackle and dead shrimp! She had no idea what kind of fish they were or that catching them while practically standing on sand was unheard of farther north.

Talking to a seasoned commercial fisherman who lived nearby, I found that the jetty had been a prime spot for catching giant jewfish, now called Goliath grouper, ranging from 90 to well over 200 pounds. Spear fishers had thinned the big fish out, but since they have been protected for the past several years, the population should be rebounding. The old fisherman also spoke of seeing big lings (cobias) caught off the end of the jetty, as well as other species considered offshore denizens. He said local legend had it that a big storm had washed enough jetty rocks offshore to form a sizable reef only a few miles out to attract and hold these fish, who then sometimes roamed in to the jetty to feed on huge schools of mullet in the channel. The close proximity of deep water probably has just as much to do with the offshore species coming in, however.

Boca Chica has long been considered the dream spot for anglers after monster-class sharks, who make pilgrimages to both the jetty and the mouth of the river. Fishing off the beach in between is also productive, and I can testify there are deep

Boca Chica Beach is almost totally undeveloped, except for these few fishing cabins near the jetty.

holes in some places between sandbars, having dropped below my waders in one— and finding it filled with frigid green water!

The beach can normally be driven in the family car, from river to jetty. The surf is amazingly clear, even when rough, and it is one of the best places on the Gulf coast for a surf angler to tangle with trophy-class quarry. Monster sharks, tarpon, snook, bull reds, and various offshore species lured close by the jetties and rock not far off the river mouth are always a possibility most months of the year. Prime time to seriously fish Boca Chica would be spring and fall; summer—which is very hot—sees a lot of beach goers; and winter will find "winter Texans" searching for shells—at least during the day.

I visited Boca Chica in March of 2007 for the first time in over thirty years to find that, amazingly, very little had changed in that time. The drive to this lonely stretch of beach goes through an often-desolate landscape, but on that trip the yucca plants were in bloom, thousands of them, many over 10 feet tall. The other thing different was the Border Patrol checkpoint, where two bored-looking agents half-heartedly checked for illegal aliens in vehicles leaving the beach.

On previous trips in the late 1970s, I had wondered why no one checked for illegal border crossings and smuggling on the only road leading from a spot where an international border could be crossed by wading most of the time, and by small boat anytime. In fact, on one of those earlier visits, I watched as three people launched a small sailing catamaran in the surf near the river mouth at dusk, headed

Fishing on Boca Chica beach. The seaweed piled at the water's edge makes fishing tough, but is not an everyday occurrence.

out on an angle toward Mexico, and returned several hours later, well after dark. Hmmm . . .

Several developers had planned big marina/canal complexes in the wetlands behind Boca Chica, but all these efforts have been successfully held off so far. In this day and age, it is unusual to see such a lovely piece of beach that is easily accessed by a paved road and has pretty much no development, nor any signs of human habitation other than a few weathered fishing shacks near the jetties. This alone makes Boca Chica a very special place, even without the international border and exceptional fishing.

Boca Chica is also a very good place to simply relax. Even though it's easy to get there, the lack of facilities keeps most casual beach visitors away. Camping is wide open, there are no restrictions on driving the beach or campfires, and portable toilets and trash cans are spaced out along the beach. In March I did encounter a tour group brought over in a large amphibious "duck" that sailed from South Padre Island or Port Isabel and crossed the Brazos Santiago Channel above the jetties. These activities may allow tourists to visit, but they do not stay very long.

At Boca Chica, besides fishing, you can sit on the jetties and watch boats head out or come in, check out the high-rises on South Padre Island across the channel, or drive to the river and wave at the anglers on the Mexican side. The sand is white and clean, the dunes are tall, and the night sky is clear and filled with stars—stars that are not dimmed by city lights or filtered through industrial smog.

On my first trip to Boca Chica, which was during winter, we camped one night at a spot between the paved access and the jetties, a break in the dunes where a sand flat flowed between tall white mountains in the bright moonlight. It was like a pristine lunar landscape, with only some scattered driftwood to break the plane. Behind the dunes, scrub brush sloped off toward South Bay, and across the beach, the surf crashed in with glowing foamy crests. With absolutely no sounds other than the waves and the crackling of a driftwood fire, a more peaceful and serene setting would be hard to imagine. I remember sitting up most of that crisp night, feeding the fire and feeling very satisfied. The memory of that night had apparently faded in thirty or so years, but it came slipping back when I drove past the spot on my recent visit to Boca Chica. It was still there, virtually unchanged—not quite as spectacular in the daytime, but still very noticeable. My soul tells me I need to see it again, at least once more in my lifetime, on another crisp, clear winter night.

The river mouth would be an interesting place to spend some time—river mouths always are. This particular river is one of the most storied in the country— heck, John Wayne chased the bad guys across it in movie after movie, and it is crossed daily by thousands of tourists and other visitors, both legal and illegal, going both ways. The land on the Mexican side of the river doesn't look much different than Texas, except for the lighthouse a little farther down the beach. Even the people and the vehicles—mostly late-model trucks made in the USA on my last visit—look much the same on both sides. Perhaps some insight into the differences and similarities between two counties separated by a river could be gained by merely sitting on the shore and absorbing the situation. If not, drive to Matamoras, cross the border, and absorb some Mexican food and culture closer at hand.

Boca Chica is the end of the Texas coast fishing story, even though it—like the whole coast—offers much more than just fishing. Texas is often described as a state of mind, and this suits our coast very well. Seafood and sand, clean water and ample sun, fun-filled resorts and desolate beaches—the Texas coast is an experience no angler or other visitor should pass up. Start at Sabine Pass and stop at Boca Chica—or jump the Rio Grande to fish the passes and rivers below the border. Soak up the sun by day, gaze at the stars at night, and enjoy the normally mild Texas winters. Enjoy, and enjoy again.

The road leading to Boca Chica has few scenic views, but in early spring yuccas by the thousands might be seen blooming, many of them well over 10 feet tall.

FISHING THE TEXAS GULF COAST

Appendix A:
Texas Saltwater Fish State Records

The data involving state record fish can be both interesting and informative. It can tell us, roughly, where the largest fish of a given species has been caught—which can help in making a decision as to where to fish. Knowing the dates these fish were caught might be an indicator of whether fishing for each species has declined. The tarpon record, for instance, was set in 2006, breaking the previous record that had stood for over thirty years. This would seem to indicate that tarpon stocks are stable or even improving. The speckled trout (spotted seatrout) record, however, was taken from an area—Baffin Bay—that is famous for large numbers of big trout but will soon have tighter catch restrictions than the rest of the Texas coast because catch surveys are showing a decline in Baffin Bay's trout numbers overall.

I have marked two records with asterisks. Since both the snook and jack crevalle records are larger than the all-tackle world records for these species, I would consider them suspect. Since the snook record was taken in 1937, when the state's fisheries science was in its infancy, it was very likely a misidentification or maybe a fish commonly called "snook" by local anglers but not a true snook as caught in Florida and Central America. The jack crevalle record is suspect because these fish seldom exceed 25 pounds in Texas waters. Since the fish was caught in January, when jack crevalles are not common in Texas waters, there is a very good chance that this was an amberjack incorrectly identified as a crevalle.

Inshore and Near-Offshore Texas State Records
(as of November 2008)

Species	Weight (Pounds)	Date	Location	Angler
Alligator gar	186.19	10/15/95	Galveston Bay	Johnny Gilbert
Atlantic croaker	5.47	4/24/02	Gulf of Mexico	Paul Straw
Atlantic stingray	10.75	7/3/94	Galveston Bay	David Anderson
Black drum	81.0	6/19/88	Gulf of Mexico	Wally Escobar
Blue catfish	42.78	5/12/05	Sabine Lake	Bob Hutchinson
Bluefish	16.62	1/11/87	Gulf of Mexico	Alex Koumonduras
Bonnethead shark	24.3	6/18/04	Gulf of Mexico	Pamela Joseph
Bull shark	508.0	7/3/94	Gulf of Mexico	Jimmy Hart
Cobia	108.44	5/9/98	Gulf of Mexico	Mike Albanese
Common snook*	52.5	1/1/37	Gulf of Mexico	Louis Rawalt
Crevalle jack*	50.25	1/26/76	Gulf of Mexico	Francis Lyon
Flathead catfish	23.32	9/6/04	Sabine Lake	Bob Hutchinson
Florida pompano	6.4	11/18/06	Lower Laguna Madre	Juan Carillo
Flounder (fly rod)	4.3	8/22/00	Lower Laguna Madre	Skipper Ray
Gafftop catfish	13.33	12/13/81	Gulf of Mexico	Herman Koenhne
Hardhead catfish	4.06	7/14/03	Corpus Christi Bay	Federico Garcia
King mackerel	79.0	8/20/06	Gulf of Mexico	Mervin Leppo
Ladyfish	4.99	8/14/05	Aransas Bay	Clint Smith
Little tunny	13.9	8/1/06	Gulf of Mexico	Brandon Shuler
Ocellated flounder	2.63	1/6/01	Galveston Bay	Mark Bond
Pompano dolphin	4.1	8/3/90	Gulf of Mexico	Tommy Gueldner
Redfish	59.5	1/30/00	Gulf of Mexico	Artie Longron
Red snapper	38.13	7/14/98	Gulf of Mexico	Jack Brumby
Roughtail stingray	241.0	9/2/91	Gulf of Mexico	Rick Jansky
Sand seatrout	6.25	2/26/72	Galveston Bay	Dennis Herrick
Sheepshead	15.25	10/17/02	Lower Laguna Madre	Wayne Gilstrap
Southern flounder	13.0	2/18/76	Galveston Bay	Herbert Endicott
Southern stingray	246.0	6/30/96	Galveston Bay	Carissa Egger
Spanish mackerel	8.74	8/15/76	Gulf of Mexico	Bobby Tarter
Spotted seatrout	15.6	5/23/02	Baffin Bay	Carl Rowland
Striped bass	28.0	1/26/91	Galveston Bay	Calvin Hinderman
Tarpon	210.7	10/4/06	Galveston Pier	Jeremy Ebert
Tripletail	33.5	6/29/84	Matagorda Bay	Edie Pruett

* See text on p. 123

Appendix B:
Texas Saltwater Fishing Regulations Overview

A fishing license with a saltwater stamp is required for both residents and nonresidents. There is a movement by NOAA Fisheries to require state-by-state licenses, but it appears that the Texas saltwater stamp will comply.

Because fisheries regulations change often, please check for updates before hitting the water.

Bag and Length Limits for Saltwater Fish

Species	Daily Bag Limit	Minimum/Maximum Length (Inches)
Black drum	5	14/30
Blue catfish	25	12/none
Flathead catfish	5	12/none
Flounder	10	14/none
Gafftop catfish	no limit	14/none
King mackerel	2	27/none
Ling (cobia)	2	37/none
Red drum	3	20/28
Red snapper	4	15/none
Sharks (all coastal)	1	53/none
Sharks (sharpnose)	5	none
Snook	1	24/28
Spanish mackerel	15	14/none
Speckled trout	10	15/25
Striped bass	5	18/none
Tarpon	1	80/none
Tripletail	3	17/none

Special Notes

One black drum over 30 inches may be retained per day and counts as part of the daily bag limit.

One red drum (redfish) over the 28-inch maximum may be retained if tagged with the red drum tag on your fishing license. When this tag is filled out and sent in, a bonus red drum tag may be issued, allowing another large fish to be kept. This fish will be additional to the daily bag limit.

One speckled trout (spotted seatrout) over the 25-inch maximum may be retained per day and counts as part of the daily limit.

These exceptions were made to allow the keeping of trophy fish that could be new state records. The special tag that was until recently required to keep a trophy tarpon may be reinstated, now that the thirty-year-old state record has been broken.

The bag limit for speckled trout in the Lower Laguna Madre and Baffin Bay may be reduced to five fish per day before this book is published.

Index

Index

About the Author

Mike Holmes has been fishing the Texas coast since the mid 1970s, starting as a long-rod surf fisherman. Over the years he has fished or visited every portion of the Texas shoreline and fished bays, rivers, bayous, and offshore. A licensed charter-boat captain since 1982, he owns and operates a restored 1962 vintage 31 Bertram express sportfisherman, lovingly updated and repowered with modern diesel engines, based in Freeport.

Capt. Holmes has been writing for local and national outdoors publications since 1979 and has seen hundreds of his articles published in over thirty magazines, including *Outdoor Life, Boating, Sportfishing, Saltwater Sportsman,* and *Marlin.* He is currently a columnist for *Southern Boating* of Fort Lauderdale, Florida, plus *Saltwater Texas* and *Texas Fish & Game.* He is an active member of the Texas Outdoor Writer's Association, Outdoor Writer's Association of America, Professional Outdoor Media Association, and Boating Writers' International, and has won many awards for his articles and columns.

Always active in fisheries conservation and management issues, Capt. Holmes has recently been appointed to his fourth two-year term on the Coastal Migratory Pelagics Advisory Panel to the Gulf of Mexico Fisheries Management Council, and is a member of the National Association of Charterboat Operators.

Capt. Holmes lives with his wife and three Catahoula leopard dogs in Oyster Creek, near Freeport.